The Vanished
TEXAS COAST

LOST PORT TOWNS, MYSTERIOUS
SHIPWRECKS AND OTHER TRUE TALES

MARK LARDAS

THE
History
PRESS

Published by The History Press
Charleston, SC
www.historypress.com

Copyright © 2021 by Mark Lardas
All rights reserved

Front cover, top: The Mexican Iron Steam Frigate Guadalupe. *Author's collection.*
Front cover, bottom: Galveston after the 1900 hurricane leveled the town.
Library of Congress. Back cover, top: Cabeza de Vaca makes an unscheduled
arrival in Texas. *Author's collection. Back cover, bottom*: The causeway linking
Galveston Island to the mainland after the 1915 hurricane. *University of
Houston Digital Library.*

First published 2021

Manufactured in the United States

ISBN 9781467149853

Library of Congress Control Number: 2021937217

Notice: The information in this book is true and complete to the best of our
knowledge. It is offered without guarantee on the part of the author or The
History Press. The author and The History Press disclaim all liability in
connection with the use of this book.

To Joanna.

CONTENTS

ACKNOWLEDGMENTS

No book is the product of a single author. Many folks helped me as I wrote and assembled this book. Those I would especially like to note include:

The Helen Hall Library in League City, which went above and beyond in providing materials from their Local History Collection and securing other material through interlibrary loan. Your local public library is a great starting point for any researcher.

Justin Parkoff of the Texas Maritime Museum, Mark Underhill, Burt Reckles, Charles Cosewith and William Wardle for providing information used in this book. Justin Parkoff provided new information about *Zavala* that led me to rewrite the ending of that chapter.

Charles Cosewith and William Wardle allowed me to use their models in illustrations. Thanks, I appreciate it.

Charles Cosewith, Mark Underhill, Justin Parkoff and William Lardas for photos used in this book.

I would also like to thank Ben Gibson, my editor at The History Press, for his assistance.

The following abbreviations indicate the sources of the illustrations used in this volume:

AC: author's collection of images
LOC: Library of Congress
POHA: Port of Houston Authority

UHDL: University of Houston Digital Archive Library
USNHHC: United States Navy Heritage and History Command.

Other photographers are listed in full.

INTRODUCTION

The Texas coast is filled with ghosts. These ghosts are not what are traditionally thought of as ghosts: haunts, the unquiet dead who do not sleep peacefully in their graves. Rather these ghosts are those of Texas history. They are the men and women, ships and events that shaped Texas history and have been forgotten over time—the people and things that made Texas what it is today, invisibly influencing Texas from its beginnings through the present. Their presence haunts Texas, sometimes for ill but more frequently for the better.

People associate Texas with cowboys and cattle, cotton and oil. Today, Texas is high-tech: the Telecom Corridor in Dallas, computers in Austin, NASA in Houston. Many think of it as a product of its land.

Yet Texas has always been influenced by the sea. For 350 years, the sea carried Texas history. It brought explorers, castaways, pirates, empresarios, immigrants and cargoes. It carried away Texas's agricultural goods, bringing wealth to the state. Before the railroad and telegraph, the sea was the quickest way to communicate with the state or for the state to communicate with the outside world.

From Texas's discovery in 1519 until after the Civil War in the 1870s, the easiest way to reach Texas was by sea. Swamps guarded its eastern approaches, as did arid plains to its north. Inhospitable deserts shield its southwest and west frontiers. The only easy access to Texas came through the Gulf Coast on its southeast. A man could cross the swamps, plains or desert by foot or on horseback but could carry little with him. You would be lucky to bring in more than the provisions required to carry you across those barriers.

You certainly could not carry the wealth of Texas out that way. Cotton, cattle and corn were valuable but carrying the quantities required for a profitable trip was not possible on horseback, by packhorse or even by wagon. Until the railroad and automobile arrived carrying these cargoes, distances greater than thirty meant they had to be carried by boat on Texas's rivers to the coast and from there to East Coast and European markets by seagoing ships.

The sea shaped Texas's destiny. It brought the first Spanish and French to Texas. It carried the Old Three Hundred to Texas. It helped Mexico gain independence from Spain. Texas's independence from Mexico was secured by sea. The Texas Navy kept Texas an independent republic even as Mexico's other breakaway states were forced back into Mexico. Later, the sea brought the Germans to Texas's Hill Country. During the Civil War, battles fought on Texas's coasts allowed Texas to remain the last unconquered part of the Confederacy. (If you ask most native Texans, Texas did not lose the Civil War so much as it decided to rejoin the Union after the rest of the Confederacy gave up.)

After the Civil War, the sea still brought Texas fortune. Galveston became one of the great immigration ports of the United States, second only to New York City. Texas's seaports boomed, the railroads fueling their growth rather than stifling it. Today, Houston is the nation's second-largest seaport. The sea's bounty also provides wealth to Texas in the form of its shrimping, fishing and offshore oil industry.

Most of this wealth was hard-won. Texas's seacoast is shallow, filled with shifting sandbars. Corpus Christi, Port Arthur, Orange and Brownsville emerged through human effort, carved out of offshore shallows. Texas's greatest seaport, Houston, is completely man-made. Even Galveston, its finest natural seaport, is largely artificial, dredged from the mud on the bottom of Galveston Harbor and Galveston Bay. Much of the spoil used to create its harbor helped raise Galveston above the sea.

This history is largely forgotten today. Most of Texas's cultural memory is landlocked. Its past is a tale of cowboy and trail drives and journeys on horseback or aboard the iron horse. Its present is associated with oil fields, high-tech industry and cutting-edge medicine. Its maritime heritage has faded to invisibility, faded and ghostlike. The Texas Rangers are remembered; the Texas Navy is forgotten. Space captures the imagination, not shipping.

This book attempts to remind Texans—and everyone—about Texas's neglected maritime heritage. I start at the beginning and go to the present. Along the way, you meet a varied cast. I reanimate the ghosts of Spanish, French and German noblemen; various pirates; and an awful lot of ordinary folks who manned the ships, loaded and unloaded them or simply came to Texas by sea. There are some businessmen, a few politicians (every tale needs villains) and quite a few naval officers, some more competent than others.

The inhabitants of Texas prior to the Texas Revolution were natives or colonists, Texians during the revolutionary era and the years of the Republic of Texas, and Texans after Texas became part of the United States. It does not matter what they called themselves, however. By whatever name, they were and remain affected by the sea and its influence on Texas, even if they do not realize it.

1

CABEZA DE VACA AND
THE DAWN OF TEXAS HISTORY

In 1628, Texas was *terra incognita*, unknown territory. Its coast had been charted in 1519 by Alonso Álvarez de Pineda, who led an expedition of four caravels departing Jamaica to skirt the Gulf Coast from the coast of Florida to modern Mexico. He got as far south as today's Veracruz before returning to Jamaica. But de Pineda never landed, except at Hernan Cortez's newly established colony of Villa Rica de la Vera Cruz. There, de Pineda received a frosty welcome. The whole of today's U.S. interior remained unexplored for another nine years. Texas was just a coastline on a nautical chart.

Texas entered recorded history as the result of an accident, a shipwreck that killed all but 4 of nearly 250 men aboard five ill-made rafts. The ghosts of over 240 members of the expedition may still haunt the Texas coast. Yet one of the four who survived, Álvar Núñez Cabeza de Vaca, returned to Spain to write an account of his adventures in the New World, including an epic trek across Texas. It was the first written account of Texas.

Cabeza de Vaca was born near Cadiz, Spain, somewhere between 1487 and 1492. His birthday and the origin of his unusual surname (Spanish for "Cow's Head") are unknown. Most of the many explanations for his surname are dubious, if colorful. He was born into a hidalgo family, minor Spanish nobility. He became a soldier in the Spanish army in his teens, after both of his parents died.

He did well as a soldier. He fought in Italy at the Battle of Ravenna in 1512. Cabeza de Vaca fought for King Charles I when the Revolt of the

A bust of Álvar Núñez Cabeza de Vaca on display at Houston's Hermann Park. Although largely forgotten by most Texans, Cabeza de Vaca remains honored by those for whom Texas history is important. *Author photograph.*

Comuneros broke out against the king in 1520 and helped defend Spain when France invaded Navarre in 1521. In 1527, the crown rewarded Cabeza de Vaca by appointing him royal treasurer on an upcoming expedition to be led by Pánfilo de Narváez.

It was an important assignment. To the king of Spain, his treasurer was the most important man in an expedition. The royal treasurer's job was to track expenditures and any money gained (through capturing treasure or simply the sale of goods produced during an expedition). The royal treasurer ensured the crown got its percentage of an expedition's profits.

Narváez played a minor role in Cortez's conquest of Mexico seven years earlier. Now he proposed sending an expedition to today's Florida to exploit its wealth, especially all the gold Narváez assumed would be found there. Charles I granted Narváez a charter assigning Narváez the right to explore, colonize and exploit the territory between Florida and Río de las Palmas. Narváez believed Río de las Palmas to be perhaps 40 to 80 miles from where he intended to land in Florida. In reality, Río de las Palmas was north of present-day Tampico, Mexico, 1,500 miles away.

The expedition began badly and ended disastrously. Narváez landed on the Gulf coast of Central Florida near Tampa Bay with five ships and four hundred men. He lost one ship almost immediately. Then he split the expedition, taking three hundred men and forty horses north and inland, seeking treasure. He ordered the men remaining aboard the ships to meet him farther north at a harbor Narváez presumed was there. There was no harbor. The ships searched for Narváez and his men for nearly a year before giving up and sailing to Mexico. Narváez and his men in Florida were stranded.

At first, things went well for the shore party. They bullied the local Natives into providing them with food and gold. The locals soon grew tired of their arrogant visitors, especially once Narváez's party reached the territory of the Apalachee, a powerful and warlike people. The Apalachee burned the Spanish out of a village they had taken. The tribe then conducted guerrilla warfare against the Spanish. Soon, the Spanish found themselves trapped. They were unable to conquer the Apalachee; their numbers and their horses were being reduced, and they were running out of food. They retreated to the seacoast to harvest oysters for food.

One man finally suggested building boats and sailing them to the "nearby" Río de las Palmas. They believed it was not far. Even if they had known the true distance to the settlement at the mouth of Río de las Palmas, they almost certainly would have followed this suggestion. Remaining would condemn them all to a lingering death. Taking to the ocean offered a chance for survival.

If they had men skilled in woodworking, they could have built ships. It was done on several occasions during the era of Spanish exploration. But only one member of their party was a carpenter. Instead, they built five forty-foot-long log rafts.

They built a forge and melted down their metal armor, objects such as spurs and even some of their weapons. They used the steel to make the saws, axes and nails needed to build the rafts. They killed their horses, smoking the meat and using the manes and tails to weave rope. They made water skins from the horsehides. They carved masts, spars and oars from local timber and patched together sails from their clothing. They boiled pine pitch for caulking and shredded palmetto leaves for oakum to stuff cracks. They raided a nearby village, carrying away 640 bushels of corn to provision their journey.

Work started on August 4, 1528. The rafts were completed by mid-September. On September 22, they set sail for Río de las Palmas. Of the 300 men who accompanied Narváez, only 242 remained. They crowded onto the five rafts, nearly fifty men per forty-by-thirty-foot raft, and set out on the Gulf. Cabeza de Vaca, as an expedition officer, commanded one of the rafts.

A model representing the appearance of the raft built by Narváez expedition members to escape Florida. Cabeza de Vaca commanded one of the five rafts. *Model by William Wardle, author photograph.*

The shallow draft rafts could sail only in the direction of the wind. The rafts floated mere inches above the water. Waves kept men wet and soaked any stores aboard—even during relatively calm weather. During storms, rollers swept over the rafts, leaving everything drenched. The water skins and food soon rotted, leaving the men without food or water.

The rafts followed the Gulf Coast. Whenever they tried to land, the Natives attacked them. Thirty days after putting off, they reached the mouth of the Mississippi. Its outflow swept the rafts out to sea. Before they regained the coast, the expedition was hit by a storm, possibly a late-season tropical storm or minor hurricane. The rafts were scattered, losing sight of the other rafts.

Over the next few days, the five rafts were driven ashore on the Texas coast. They wrecked on the upper Texas coast from present-day Galveston Island to the Matagorda Peninsula. All aboard three rafts, including the one commanded by Narváez, drowned or were killed by local Natives shortly after landing. On November 6, Cabeza de Vaca's raft landed on what is today Follet's Island, across San Luis Pass from Galveston Island. Forty survivors made it ashore. Exploring, they found they were on an island. They named the island Isla de Malhado (Isle of Misfortune).

They soon discovered it was inhabited. The Natives exchanged food for beads and bells. A few days after landing, the Spanish refloated their raft. It swamped almost immediately after launching, drowning several aboard and leaving the rest with nothing. The survivors surrendered themselves to the Natives, who took them in. While living among the Natives, they discovered a second raft had come ashore on the same island with another forty survivors. They too had lost their raft and all their possessions.

The Spanish were forced to live on the hospitality of the Natives. The Natives used the Spanish as unpaid labor, giving the Spanish the least desirable tasks. Food shortages developed during late winter. By the spring of 1529, only Cabeza de Vaca and fourteen other Spanish wrecked on Isla de Malhado were still alive. Illness and starvation had killed the rest.

For the next four years, Cabeza de Vaca and the dwindling band of Spanish survivors lived among the Natives, effectively as slaves. The

The five rafts of the Narváez expedition were washed ashore on the Texas coast in an arc from Galveston Island to Matagorda Peninsula during a late-season tropical storm or weak hurricane. The crews lost most of their possessions when the rafts ran aground. *AC.*

survivors were split up. A dozen attempted to walk to Mexico. Nine of these died. Three others were captured and enslaved by the coastal Coahuiltecan Indians. Cabeza de Vaca and two others remained with the Karankawas on Galveston Island. Cabeza de Vaca became a trader, trading coastal seashells and pearls for inland bison skins and red ochre. He also served as a healer, earning food by curing the sick.

After four years, Cabeza de Vaca persuaded the only surviving Spaniard with him, Lope de Oviedo, to abandon Isla de Malhado and strike inland. When they reached Matagorda Bay, they encountered the Quevene Indians (possibly the Cujanes, a Karankawan group). When the Natives threatened the pair, de Oviedo fled, disappearing from history. But although the Quevene behaved threateningly, they did not harm Cabeza de Vaca. Instead, they told Cabeza de Vaca about three other surviving members of the Narváez expedition living with another tribe, the Mariames. They transported Cabeza de Vaca across Matagorda Bay.

There, Cabeza de Vaca continued until he reached the "River of Nuts" (today's Guadalupe River). He joined the other three, Alonso del Castillo, Andrés Dorantes de Carranza and Estevanico. Del Castillo and Dorantes, like Cabeza de Vaca, were hidalgos. Estevanico was an enslaved Moor brought to the New World by Dorantes. These were three survivors of the twelve who left Isla de Malhado. They had been enslaved by the Mariames. They thought Cabeza de Vaca had died.

By joining them, Cabeza de Vaca accepted captivity among the Mariames. The Natives treated all four as slaves. It did reunite him with the remaining survivors of the party. The four, known as the "Ragged Castaways," remained among the Mariames for another eighteen months. After six months, the four were split into two parties, with Cabeza de Vaca and Dorantes in one village and Del Castillo and Estevanico in another. They were brought together when the two villages united for an annual fishing expedition on the coast.

The castaways took advantage of this to escape the Mariames. One night in early September, each man independently snuck away and headed south. They reunited by the end of the month. Striking inland, the four continued as a party.

Luck continued favoring them. The next Natives they encountered, the Avavare, were friendly. Cabeza de Vaca was accepted as a powerful healer among them, even though he knew little of medicine. He combined the Native custom of blowing on the ill and basic first aid for injuries with a good deal of Catholic prayer. At one point, Cabeza de Vaca removed an arrowhead lodged above the heart of a Native. Either good fortune or divine

The cover page of the second edition of Cabeza da Vaca's memoirs of the Narváez expedition, published in 1542. The memoirs were the first mention of Texas in printed word and a groundbreaking work in ethnology, the study of people. *AC.*

intervention led most of those he treated to recover. Cabeza de Vaca would later write that any cures came from God and not from himself.

Accompanied by Native guides, the four traveled south, crossing the Nueces and Rio Grande Rivers. They began traveling west toward the Pacific when they reached the San Juan River in Mexico. Eventually, they reached the Rio Grande near the Big Bend, following it to roughly the current location of El Paso. Then the four crossed the Sonora Desert. Around Christmas in 1535, they saw evidence of other Europeans: a horseshoe nail and a belt buckle. Finally, they encountered other Spanish explorers and were taken to San Miguel de Culiacán on Mexico's west coast.

From there, they traveled to Mexico City, arriving in July 1536. Del Castillo and Dorantes settled there, marrying rich widows and ending their travels. Cabeza de Vaca returned to Spain in 1837. In the 1540s, he was made governor of what is today Paraguay. Before that appointment, he wrote his memoirs of his travels between 1528 and 1536.

His memoirs were first published in 1542 with the title of *La relación y comentarios* ("the account and commentaries"). It has since been republished in multiple languages under a variety of titles. The book was the first written account that discussed Texas. It was a classic and pioneering work. Today, Cabeza de Vaca is considered Texas's first ethnologist. His description of the lives of the tribes of the Natives of the Texas coast is one of the earliest examples of ethnology, the study of characteristics of peoples and the differences and relationships between them. He brought Texas into the history books with this work.

Unfortunately, the rest of his life progressed poorly. His life among the Texas Natives gave him a natural sympathy of all the indigenous inhabitants of the Americas. As governor, he became a champion of Indian rights. His efforts to protect the Guatanis of Paraguay from exploitation by the Spanish settlers led to his deposition by the other Spanish settlers. He was sent back to Spain in chains, barred from ever returning to the New World and tried and convicted on thirty-two charges of abuse of power.

His sentence of five years penal service in North Africa was commuted and he lived out the rest of his life in Spain. Regardless, his memory is still revered in Texas. A giant of Texas history, Álvar Núñez Cabeza de Vaca remains one of the benign ghosts of the Texas coast.

2

THE LOST TREASURE FLEET

On April 9, 1554, four ships set sail from San Juan de Ulúa (today's Veracruz) in Mexico for the Cuban port of Havana. In Havana, they were to join a convoy bound for Seville in Spain. This annual *flota* (fleet) carried the cargo of silver, gold and other precious cargoes sailing annually from Spain's New World colonies home to the mother country.

Three of the four ships, *San Esteban*, *Espíritu Santo* and *Santa María de Yciar*, never arrived. The fourth, *San Andrés*, reached port so badly damaged that it never sailed again. Of the over four hundred crew and passengers aboard the ship, fewer than a quarter survived this voyage. Less than half of those survivors lived to eventually return to Spain, their ultimate destination when they left Veracruz.

Instead, they left the ghosts of three hundred unquiet dead and their mark on Texas history. Their story, largely forgotten over the next one hundred years, generated legends of buried treasure on the Texas coast that lingered to the twentieth century. Only then did the legend prove real.

The ships had left Spain eighteen months earlier, part of a fleet of fifty-four vessels. Sixteen were bound for Mexico. Only five were supposed to return to Spain, including the four that set forth on April 9. The rest were to be scrapped in the New World to provide resources for the growing colony Spain planted at San Juan de Ulúa. The returning ships should have departed Mexico in April 1553 but were delayed through a combination of bad weather and bad fortune. Only *San Pedro*, the fifth ship scheduled to return to Spain, managed to depart for Havana in 1553.

The Spanish sent annual colonization fleets to their American New World colonies and retrieved the silver, gold and other wealth their colonies generated through an annual treasure fleet that sailed from Havana to Seville in the fall. A fleet from today's Veracruz set off annually across the Gulf of Mexico to Havana to join the homeward-bound flota. *AC.*

The captains of the remaining ships were supposed to await naval escorts before leaving port. They knew if they delayed much longer they would miss the 1554 flota sailing for Spain from Havana and would be stuck in the New World for yet another year. They decided to leave in company, unescorted. *San Andrés*'s master, Antonio Corz, was elected captain-general of this improvised flota, probably because he was viewed as the most experienced captain.

The ships were carrying a literal king's ransom. The cargo included silver coins, plate silver, gold, cochineal, resins, sugar and cow hides. The four ships carried ninety-six thousand pounds of silver and gold, worth between $20 million and $30 million today. The ships also carried at least twenty tons of cochineal, used to create a scarlet dye. This added a minimum of $10 million to the value of the cargo carried. In all, the cargo carried was worth the equivalent of $46 million in today's dollars.

It was the annual production of Mexico and Spain's colonies in mainland Central and South America. Silver from Peru went up the Pacific coast to Panama. It then moved overland to Nombres de Dios on the Gulf Coast and north to Veracruz in coastal vessels.

Also aboard were passengers returning to Spain with their private riches after making their fortunes in the New World. These included families with many women and children. The passengers included Dona Catalina de Ribera, Juan Ponce de Leon's widow.

At first all went well. The previous year's ill luck seemed gone. The ships had reached the northern shore of Cuba and were almost within sight of Havana when they got caught by a late equinoctial gale.

The ships of the era were not weatherly. Sixteenth-century ships lacked fore-and-aft sails now common on sailing ships. These allow modern sailing ships to steer close to the wind. Ships used to cross the Atlantic were either carracks or galleons. They had three to four masts. Except for a lateen sail or two on the after masts, all of the sails these ships carried were square sails with yards perpendicular to the ship's length. Instead of the triangular jibs on the bow, used to help steer ships today, sixteenth-century vessels had a square sail, called a spritsail, hung under the bowsprit. It could not be used in rough seas. To provide additional accommodation, these ships had high forecastles and stern castles, sometimes towering four to five levels above the deck. While useful in combat, they served as giant, fixed sails.

Even under minimal sail, steering a course perpendicular to a strong wind risked rolling the ship onto its beam ends, capsizing it. The ships could not turn into the wind and wait it out. The wind would push them backward.

Eventually, the crew would lose control, and the ship would broach to one side or the other, broadside to the wind and capsize. They could not even abandon ship. Ships boats would be swamped in the stormy seas. All they could do was run before the wind until the gale ended.

The storm blew the four ships back across the Gulf of Mexico. The gale kept up until they were off today's Texas coast. They ran out of sea room before the storm ended. *San Esteban*, *Espíritu Santo* and *Santa María de Yciar* ran ashore on then-unnamed South Padre Island, south of today's Texas port city of Corpus Christi. *San Andrés* managed to claw off the lee shore and avoid wrecking.

Released from the storm's iron grip, *San Andrés* crawled back to Havana, arriving in a sinking state, reporting the disaster befalling its companions. Its cargo was unloaded and transferred to another ship headed for Spain. *San Andrés* was scrapped.

The other three ships were wrecked on the desolate shores of one of South Texas's barrier islands, barren scrub-covered sand dunes offering no food or water. They landed within two and a half miles of each other, with *San Esteban* farthest north and *Santa María de Yciar* farthest south. Just over three hundred people were aboard when the ships wrecked. Deep-draft ships, they ran aground some distance from shore. To reach shore, survivors had to struggle through water too deep to wade to reach shore. It was an age when few, including mariners, knew how to swim. Only half to one-third of the ships' crews and passengers made it to shore alive. One-third of these survivors were women and children.

When the weather calmed, the survivors salvaged food and drinking water from the ships and one ship's boat from *San Esteban*. Reaching Veracruz in an open boat required a risky voyage over the Gulf of Mexico. One boat could carry only a fraction of the survivors. *San Esteban*'s master, Francisco del Huerto, resolved to do just that. With fifteen to thirty sailors, he set off for Veracruz. The rest, perhaps one hundred, were supposed to await rescue from Veracruz.

Del Huerto succeeded in sailing an open boat nearly six hundred nautical miles to San Juan de Ulúa. A rescue mission left on June 6. By the time they reached the wrecks, one man, Francisco Vazquez, remained on South Padre Island. Vazquez explained that the survivors departed a few days after *San Esteban*'s boat sailed. The Native Karankawas began harassing the castaways. They decided remaining by the ships was too dangerous. They chose to walk overland to Spanish settlements in Mexico. With only a fuzzy knowledge of geography, they assumed the nearest Spanish colony was only

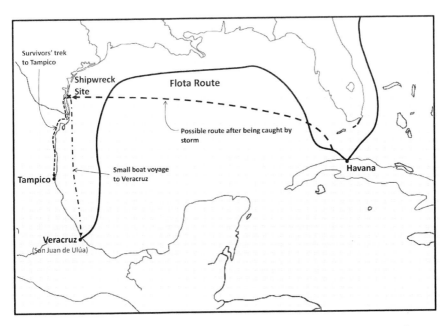

In 1554, the Mexico flota got caught by gales that blew them back across the Gulf of Mexico to wreck on the Texas coast. One group of survivors made Veracruz by ship's boat. The rest set off to march to Tampico, as shown on this map. *Author map.*

a few days hard walking. Valquez abandoned the group early and returned to the dunes, hiding until help arrived.

In reality, the nearest settlement was really five hundred miles away, near modern Tampico. The walk became a death march. Survivors had little in the way of supplies or clothes; they could take only what they could carry. They had weapons, including crossbows, which outranged the Karankawas' bows. Regardless, the Karankawas continued harassing survivors as they trekked south. Sometimes the Karankawas offered to trade fish with survivors, often using the swap sessions as opportunities to enter the Spanish camp and then attack. Stragglers who fell out from the march were usually killed by the Natives. Two were stripped of their clothes and allowed to return to the castaways.

The rest of the survivors decided that meant the Indians wanted only their clothes. Hoping to be left alone, they surrendered them. The Karankawas continued harassing them. The naked survivors were exposed to sun and mosquitoes. The surviving women, ashamed of being naked, were permitted to walk ahead of the men with their children to protect their modesty. The Karankawas attacked and killed these undefended women.

Sixteenth-century Spanish
ships had high forecastles
and sterncastles. They
lacked fore-and-aft sails,
allowing them to sail into
the wind. When the wind
blew hard, these ships
could only run before them.
*Model by William Wardle,
author photograph.*

When the castaways reached the Rio Grande, the river was too deep to ford. They built rafts from driftwood. The raft fell apart during the crossing and the Spanish lost their crossbows and most of their remaining weapons. The Spanish men who survived the crossing were soon killed by the emboldened Natives.

There was only one survivor. Marcos de Mena, a Dominican lay brother, was left for dead after being shot by seven arrows. After a night's sleep, he recovered enough to resume moving south. After traveling four days without food or water, he reached the Pánuco River. Friendly Indians found him and took him to Tampico. Thirty years later, he wrote an account of the journey, published after his death.

If the castaways were gone from South Padre Island, the treasure carried by the ships was not. The rescue mission was followed up almost immediately by a salvage mission. In July, six ships newly arrived in Mexico from Spain were sent to the wreck site to salvage as much of the cargo as could be recovered. The sugar, cochineal and hides were ruined by seawater, but the three wrecks held around seventy-two thousand pounds of precious metals.

By the time the salvage fleet arrived, only *San Esteban* had parts of its hull above water. Some men began removing its cargo as the rest of the fleet began searching for the other two wrecks. They found them by dragging—towing a weighted rope between two boats until it snagged on the underwater hulls. The *Espíritu Santo* and *Santa María de Yciar* were soon found and marked.

A camp was set up on the beach at South Padre Island. Over the next three months, salvage efforts continued. Free divers recovered what they could find from the submerged ships. A storm sank one salvage vessel but uncovered some treasure lost in *Santa María de Yciar*. The Spanish recovered 35,805 pounds of silver and gold. (The total was very carefully weighed on arrival at Veracruz.) That was believed to be only 41 percent of what was there. The rest remained lost in the sands off South Padre Island.

The Spanish never returned, keeping the location of the wrecks secret. They had no intention of advertising the presence of nearly fifty thousand pounds of silver and gold that might attract unwanted English, French and Dutch adventurers to a remote patch of Spanish-clamed coastline uninhabited by Europeans.

Eventually, everyone, including the Spanish, forgot the three wrecks. Those involved died off, and the secret died with them. Rumors of treasure ships sunk off the Texas coast remained, but most reasonable people though those were just fantastic tales. Padre Island was well off the treasure ship lanes. Many put them into the same category as ghost stories told around a bonfire while camping on South Padre Island—entertaining but unlikely.

Forgetfulness ended in the 1950s. A new harbor was completed at Port Mansfield in 1956. To improve access to it, a cut was dredged across South Padre Island in 1957. Proving Murphy's Law, the cut's route went smack over the forgotten grave of *Santa María de Yciar*. A suction dredge was used. Suddenly, hoses began spewing silver coins and ancient wood into the spoil. Examination revealed the coins to be sixteenth-century Spanish doubloons, not twentieth-century eagle silver dollars. By then, *Santa María de Yciar* had been destroyed. The coins and one of its anchors were all that could be salvaged.

The discovery renewed interest in long-forgotten legends of the 1554 wrecks. Two Spanish treasure ships were still out there. Locals began searching for them. In 1964, a sport diver found *Espritu Santo* and spent two years exploring it. In 1967, a private company, Plataro, Limited, began excavating the site. Uninterested in its history, seeking only the gold and silver in it, the company began scouring the wreck site with hydraulic pumps to uncover the metals. It recovered five hundred metal objects before the State of Texas stopped the company.

The remains of the ships were rediscovered in the 1950s through 1970s. While *Santa María de Yciar* was destroyed in the process of discovery, the other two were excavated. Many of the finds are on display at the Corpus Christy Museum of Science and History, including this gold and silver recovered from *San Esteban*. *William Lardas photo.*

In 1960, the Supreme Court ruled that Texas owned all offshore territory up to 10.35 miles (four Spanish leagues) from its coast. The state asserted that state law, not U.S. law, applied to offshore salvage in Texas waters. A long court battle ensued, which Texas eventually won. Plataro returned its finds. But the dig destroyed the archaeological value of the *Espritu Santo* site.

San Esteban remained. The third time proved the charm. *San Esteban's* site was discovered and the ship properly excavated, one of the first formal excavations of a sixteenth-century Spanish ship. Some silver and gold were found, but *San Esteban's* real treasure turned out to be the knowledge it provided about sixteenth-century ships and shipbuilding and life in sixteenth-century colonial Spain, both ashore and at sea. The wreck proved a virtual time machine.

Today, the story of the 1554 wrecks is now known. Artifacts from the disaster are on display at the Corpus Christi Museum of Science and History.

As for the treasure from *San Andrés*? It proved almost as ill-fortuned as that of its companions. The ship it was loaded onto wrecked off the coast of Portugal. Of the 375,000 pesos it carried, only 150,000, roughly 40 percent, were salvaged and got back to Seville. It was a bad year for Phillip of Spain.

3

LA SALLE'S FORGOTTEN COLONY

Every Texas schoolchild is taught that six flags have flown over Texas. Five are obvious. Spain long ruled the part of the New World that became Texas. Mexico replaced Spain when it declared its independence. Texas became independent from Mexico, formed its own republic, joined the United States, seceded, became part of the Confederacy and then resumed its allegiance to the U.S. flag. But where did the French flag come from? And why is it always shown as gold lilies on a white field instead of the tricolor associated with France today?

The answers lie in a brief, accidental and ephemeral occupation of a small corner of the Texas coast by a doomed collection of French colonists, a Gallic reprise of the Roanoke Colony in the Gulf of Mexico. It lasted less than four years before disappearing, leaving a ghost town, fleeting memories and the opportunity to claim France as one of the six nations that has held sovereignty over Texas.

The colony France planted in Texas had its origins in a plan developed by René-Robert Cavelier, Sieur de La Salle. He was born René-Robert Cavelier in Rouen, Normandy, France, in 1643 to a gentry family. He studied with the Jesuits, a Catholic religious order, taking initial orders to join the Society of Jesuits in 1660 at age seventeen. He immigrated to New France (today's Quebec) in 1666 to join his older brother, a Suplican priest. Instead of following his brother into the priesthood, René-Robert requested release from his religious vows. He was then granted a *seigneurie* (a manor) on Montreal Island, making him a *Sieur* (lord), adding "de La Salle" to describe what he was the lord of.

La Salle set up a village and started making land grants. After several years playing lord of the manor, he got bored. In 1669, he set out to explore new lands in North America, seeking what is known today as the Ohio River in hopes of seeking a path to the "Vermillion Sea" and China.

He spent the next ten years exploring. He ranged the inland rivers and lakes of North America, including expeditions through the St. Lawrence and Mississippi watersheds. La Salle established some of France's earliest Great Lakes forts. His most noted accomplishment was a trip down the Mississippi, starting in Illinois and ending at its mouth in modern Louisiana. (La Salle

René-Robert Cavelier, Sieur de La Salle. This image shows him late in life, shortly before sailing to Texas from France. *AC.*

named Louisiana to honor France's then-reigning king, Louis XIV. He also named the Mississippi River the Rivière de Colbert for France's first minister of state.) After his return, he journeyed to France in 1683 to sell a marvelous idea.

La Salle proposed establishing a colony at the mouth of the Mississippi River. It was uninhabited by Europeans. That meant it could be grabbed. Although the Spanish had explored the Mississippi earlier, La Salle's exploration gave France an equal claim on the territory. A French colony at the mouth of the Mississippi would give France effective control of the Mississippi River basin, just as surely as Montreal gave France control of the waters that poured into the St. Lawrence. Britain, then France's bitterest rival, had established colonies on North America's Eastern Seaboard. If France controlled the Mississippi and St. Lawrence basins, it would pen up British expansion to east of the Appalachian Mountains.

The king approved the plan. He authorized an expedition of three ships, *Jolie*, a thirty-six-gun warship; *l'Amiable;* and *Saint François,* to carry stores. Additionally, King Louis donated *La Belle*, a ship intended to carry supplies down the Mississippi.

The initial plan was to start from France's Great Lakes possessions, assemble *La Belle* (which was to have crossed the ocean disassembled in one of the storeships) and move colonists and supplies down the Mississippi to Louisiana. But the expedition kept growing, until it eventually reached three hundred colonists. With that the plan changed. The expedition would go to

Port de Paix, a French colony on Hispaniola opposite Tortuga. There they would resupply with food and water and sail to the mouth of the Mississippi. Because of the need for extra storage, *La Belle* was assembled in France and sailed the Atlantic with the other three ships.

The four ships left La Rochelle on July 24, 1684. Things started going wrong almost at once. Four days after sailing, a storm caught the ships, and *Jolie* lost its bowsprit. The ships returned to La Rochelle for repairs, departing again on August 1.

Bad luck continued dogging the expedition. It crossed the Atlantic without stopping at Madeira to water, due to La Salle's insistence on making up lost time. It engendered bad feelings between La Salle and the officers of *Jolie*, on which he was sailing. They had private goods aboard they wished to trade at Madeira. The ships became becalmed and then ran into a hurricane. Before they reached Port de Paix, a Spanish privateer snapped up *Saint François*, with all the stores it contained.

Instead of landing at Port de Paix, at the insistence of *Jolie*'s captain, Taneguy le Gallois de Beaujeu, they bypassed it, making landfall at Petit Goave, a French colony on the southwest peninsula of Hispaniola. They arrived on September 27, fifty-eight days after leaving La Rochelle. The change had fatal consequences.

Petit Goave was smaller than Port de Paix. Supplies were harder to get and more expensive. Additionally, La Salle carried neither money nor letters of credit. Resupply had been arranged by the crown at Port de Paix. More importantly, while it was easy to sail directly to the Gulf of Mexico's North American coast from Port de Paix, from Petit Goave, it was quicker and safer for the ships to sail south of Cuba before sailing north to the American continent.

La Salle became ill, further stalling progress. Moreover, storms and calms separated the four ships during the Atlantic crossing, and *Jolie* and La Salle had to wait for them to arrive. They straggled in five days later, on October 2. Not until October 20 did they learn of *Saint François*'s loss. The blow was devastating because *Saint François* carried most of the expedition's provisions, as well as its cooking pots and dishes.

Regardless, the expedition pressed on, obtaining more food locally, some of which was donated. The long wait led some members of the expedition to abandon it. They joined several of the ships run by French buccaneers operating out of Petit Goave. La Salle engaged a local buccaneer as the expedition's navigator to guide them to and along the American coast. Although the man had extensive knowledge of the waters in and around the

La Salle's Landing in Texas (reduced fac-simile from Hennepin).

La Salle's colony unloaded in Texas with great hopes. Unfortunately, they landed four hundred miles west of their intended destination of the mouth of the Mississippi River. Shown in this engraving are *Joly* and *Amiable*. AC.

Gulf of Mexico, it was not as extensive as he claimed. The three ships of the expedition finally quitted Petit Goave on November 25, 1684.

It took seventeen days to reach Cape Saint Antoine on the western tip of Cuba, although a few days of that time were spent hunting on the Isle of Pines between Petit Goave and Cape Saint Antoine. They then sailed north to find the Gulf Coast. On December 28, they finally sighted land, reaching North America sixteen days after leaving sight of Cuba.

There was a problem. They were over one hundred miles west of the mouth of the Mississippi. They thought they had made landfall well east of the Mississippi. Unknown to their pilot, the currents in the Gulf of Mexico between the western tip of Cuba and the North American coast had a slight drift westward. Few people approached the coast from that direction, so no one was aware of it.

It was a time when accurate clocks did not exist and longitude was impossible to accurately fix at sea. A compass course and dead reckoning (the estimated speed of the ship times the hours—as measured by a sandglass—traveled) was used to determine position. The unaccounted current left La Salle's ships 150 to 200 miles west of where they thought they would be. Worse still, while everyone agreed they missed the landfall due to a current, they assumed the current had pushed them east. They concluded that they made landfall somewhere on what is now the western panhandle of Florida.

The three ships began sailing west, searching for the mouth of the Mississippi. It was bound to be within two days sailing. Five days later, they finally made landfall. There was no river and only flat pastureland. They were in far western Louisiana and more convinced than ever that they had landed well east of the Mississippi. They continued sailing west for another two and a half weeks.

They passed the mouth of the Sabine River, Galveston Bay and then the Brazos and Colorado Rivers. The outflow at none of these rivers matched what La Salle remembered from his canoe voyage down the Mississippi. Nor were they wide enough. Finally, after passing Matagorda Bay, La Salle had enough. He decided Matagorda Bay kind of sort of looked the Mississippi's mouth, and he had obviously misremembered the flow of water produced. Besides, if they did not land soon, the colonists would be out of supplies and it would be too late to start preparing that year's crops.

In February, he began landing the colonists at Matagorda Bay. A settlement was established off Garcitas Creek in what is now Victoria County, Texas. If things had been going wrong before, La Salle's misfortunes began multiplying, as if earlier misfortunes were hatching new ones. On February 20, 1685, *l'Amiable* ran aground in today's Pass Cavallo, with the loss of much of its stores.

Then in March, Beaujeu decided it was time for *Jolie* to head home. His instructions were to remain with La Salle only until the colony was established. Since La Salle and his colonists were well on their way to completing a

La Salle set out with seventeen men to march overland to French settlements on the Mississippi or the Great Lakes. He never made it out of Texas. He was ambushed and killed by two members of his party. *AC.*

temporary fort on Matagorda Island and had started building the Garcitas Creek settlement, Beaujeu felt he had done his duty. Those orders had not anticipated the loss of *l'Amiable* or *Saint François*, leaving only the small *La Belle* for maritime communications. But Beaujeu's first responsibility was to *Jolie*, and *l'Amiable*'s loss underscored the danger of keeping *Jolie* in a shallow open anchorage, unprotected against Gulf storms.

Had relations between Beaujeu and La Salle been better, Beaujeu could have stretched his orders. But both men wanted to be done with the other.

Beaujeu departed with La Salle's blessing. He also had with him a number of colonists who had grown disenchanted with the enterprise and La Salle's leadership. Among these was Minet, the expedition's royally appointed cartographer and engineer, with whom La Salle had also quarreled.

This left La Salle only 180 of the original 300 colonists. Among these were a dozen women (two of whom were married), two families with seven children and a number of boys in their mid-teens. Within a few months the colonists had thrown up a two-story house built from timbers salvaged from *l'Amiable* and five mud-and-lath huts, into which the colonists crowded.

Although a child was born in the colony, departures far outnumbered arrivals. Colonists were soon dying due to overwork, malnutrition and disease. They also managed to alienate the Karankawa Natives living near the colony, to the point of open warfare.

Instead of governing his colony, La Salle spent most of his time exploring the surrounding territory. La Salle left on the first of these scouts in October 1685. While he was gone, in early February 1686, *La Belle*, the last remaining ship, ran aground and was lost. The loss was due to carelessness and poor leadership. It left the colonists trapped in Texas.

By January 1687, only forty colonists remained alive. La Salle, finally realizing he was nowhere near the Mississippi, decided the only remaining hope lay in contacting French settlements on the Mississippi or Great Lakes and getting a rescue mission mounted. He left the settlement with the sixteen fittest men on January 19, 1687, to march however long it took to get help.

He had less than two months to live. On March 19, he was shot in the back by a disenchanted member of his party. By then, the group was east of the Navasota River. The party fractured. Some of the seventeen joined Indian tribes in the area. The three who plotted the assassination disappeared. Six managed to reach French North American settlements and reached France. There, a rescue expedition was organized.

By then, it was too late for the colonists. They held on for nearly two years, growing weaker while waiting for rescue. Then during the twelve days of Christmas in 1688–89, the Karankawa struck. Feigning friendship, they gained access to the settlement and massacred all the adults, male and female. Five children were adopted by Karankawas and remained alive.

The Spanish heard rumors of a French settlement on the Texas shores claimed by Spain. They sent ships and army troops seeking it. In April 1867, two Spanish ships sent searching found the wreck of *La Belle* in Matagorda Bay and fragments from *l'Amiable* in nearby Pass Cavallo. Two years later, an overland expedition discovered the abandoned ruins of the settlement.

When the Spanish arrived at the site of La Salle's colony, they demolished it and buried the cannon there. This was one of La Salle's cannon, still aboard *la Belle* when it sank and now on display at the Bullock Museum in Austin, Texas. *William Lardas photograph.*

They recovered the five surviving children and found several men who had left with La Salle and chose to live among the Indians. The Spanish pulled down the ruins, burying the cannon at the colony, obliterating its location. They evacuated the children to Mexico and removed the remaining Frenchmen. By 1690, only ghosts and memories remained of La Salle's grand dream of a Gulf Coast colony.

4

THE SHIPWRECK
OF LAFITTE'S DREAMS

One of the most romantic figures of Texas maritime history is Jean Lafitte. He is best remembered today as a pirate who preyed in the Gulf of Mexico and Caribbean. He is especially well known for assisting the United States during the War of 1812's Battle of New Orleans. In Texas, he is remembered for his attempt to set up a pirate colony on Galveston Island between 1817 and 1820.

In reality, Lafitte spent relatively little time as a pirate. He spent most of his career as a smuggler, a fence and a slave trader, often combining the three, buying stolen slaves who he smuggled into the United States. Lafitte also worked as a spy, often simultaneously employed by competing sides during the revolutions that wracked Spanish America following the end of the Napoleonic Wars. Other than that, and his constant double-dealing, his was a really great guy. His memory remains one of the historic ghosts on the Texas coast.

Jean Lafitte's origins and early history are shrouded and uncertain. The best guess is that Jean and his older brother, Pierre, were born near Bordeaux, France, in the 1770s. Their father appears to have been a prosperous merchant. The family fortunes appear to have declined during the French Revolution. (Bordeaux was a Royalist region.) With little opportunity in France, brothers Pierre and Jean came to the New World, relocating to the French colony of San Dominique possibly as early as 1794, but they were certainly there by 1802.

A popular nineteenth-century engraving of Jean Lafitte. Lafitte has an outsized and romantic reputation in Texas. Although he was occasionally a pirate, more often, he made money smuggling slaves and selling stores to other pirates. *AC.*

They chose poorly. San Dominique, on the western end of Hispaniola, had been France's richest American colony prior to the French Revolution. It was convulsed by slave rebellions and invasions throughout the 1790s. France attempted to put down the breakaway slave nation that had emerged there in the 1790s once the 1801 Peace of Amiens opened the Atlantic to France again. But France and Britain were once again at war by 1803. Pretty soon, the French army was chased out of San Dominique by an army of Black former slaves. San Dominique's new rulers began massacring the remaining white French in the former colony. The surviving white people, including Jean and Pierre, fled to New Orleans.

The Laffites (as they then spelled their names) arrived in New Orleans just before France sold New Orleans to the United States as part of the Louisiana Purchase. The brothers decided to stay. They probably had little choice. They likely had no other options.

They were merchants in Bordeaux and San Dominique and set themselves up as merchants in Louisiana, at first setting up a trading post at Baton Rouge. While now part of the state of Louisiana, in 1802, Baton Rouge was still claimed by Spain. The border of the Louisiana Territory was still in doubt.

The brothers were soon into very dodgy trading. They felt they had to be. There were lots of French merchants in Louisiana before the refugees from San Dominique began arriving and even more once merchants, like the Lafittes (as they began spelling their name once the United States took over), began fleeing San Dominique. The brothers were among the last to arrive at Louisiana from the former French colony and lacked opportunities to fill more legitimate market sectors. The most lucrative opportunity available to the brothers was purchasing and selling goods taken by privateers, or rather, those who claimed to be privateers.

A privateer was a ship whose captain had a letter of marque issued by a belligerent nation authorizing the capture of ships owned by or carrying cargoes to its enemies. Captured ships and cargoes became property of the crew capturing it once the prize ship was properly condemned in an admiralty court. It was a long-held practice recognized by all nations in the early 1800s. (The U.S. Constitution authorizes Congress to issue letters of marque and reprisal as one of its enumerated powers.)

In theory, privateering permitted civilian owners of commercial ships to recover losses incurred by enemy action. It was a form of do unto others as they do unto you. It allowed a regulated way for civilian ships to arm themselves during times of war to be able to resist capture. It was also believed to provide a nucleus of trained man-o'-war sailors for use by national navies. (The Royal Navy often impressed—drafted—sailors aboard privateers when it encountered a British privateer, taking crewmen who lacked certificates of exemption from impressment.)

In practice, privateering often led to piracy, simple theft on the high seas. This was especially true in a revolutionary era. Multiple governments began popping up and issuing letters of marque to anyone who applied for one. A clever (and unscrupulous) captain might get letters of marque from multiple nations—including those at war with each other. This increased the opportunities for prizes. (You had to be careful about which ports you sent the prizes to for condemnation, and if you got caught with the wrong letter of marque, you would be imprisoned or hanged.)

Admiralty courts of revolutionary nations (including France) were often inattentive about the nationality of ships captured by privateers carrying letters of marque they issued. The court received a percentage of the value of the prize condemning prizes offered a way to fill national treasuries. The result was innocent ships were frequently condemned. Plus, some privateers used dodgy drumhead admiralty courts set up by those claiming to be representatives of a revolutionary government.

Cargoes thus obtained had to be disposed of quickly before representatives of legitimate governments like Great Britain or the United States got wind of an illegitimate prize. They were sold cheap to merchants who bought the goods with few questions asked—merchants like Pierre and Jean Lafitte.

The brothers sold these stolen goods at a markup in New Orleans at prices considerably lower than market. The Lafittes' profit margins were improved because they smuggled the goods past customs, avoiding import fees and duties. Within a few years of arriving, the brothers had a lucrative business fencing stolen goods. After the 1808 Embargo Act stopped direct importation into New Orleans, the brothers set up a one-stop shop for privateers in Louisiana's Barataria Bay, selling supplies to privateers

The ruins of Lafitte's Galveston Island town of Campeche. Lafitte was forced to leave Galveston by the U.S. Navy, although he was allowed months to make preparations. He burned the fort and building when he left. *AC.*

and purchasing their cargoes and prize ships and forwarding what was purchased to New Orleans.

After the War of 1812 started, the brothers obtained letters of marque from the U.S. government. Jean ran the privateers, while Pierre minded Barataria Bay. Of course, some of the Baratarians preyed on Spanish shipping (allied to Britain but with which the United States was not at war) using French letters of marque. Using various shell-game tactics, the brothers kept the U.S. government from getting its share of even British prizes. Tired of dealing with pirates masquerading as privateers, the U.S. government raided Barataria Bay in 1812, arresting both brothers and twenty-five associates and seizing all their goods.

The brothers made bail and then skipped. Pierre was rearrested, but Jean escaped. Then Jean assisted the United States at the Battle of New Orleans, manning the artillery there with his pirates. Following the U.S. victory at New Orleans in February 1815, Jean Lafitte obtained a full pardon for prior criminal activities.

By then, the brothers had been smugglers and pirates for a dozen years. There was more privateering than ever in the Caribbean and Gulf of Mexico due to the independence movements that erupted during the Napoleonic Wars. Spanish colonies rebelled against the French-run

Spanish government when Napoleon put his brother on the Spanish throne. Later, they decided they would rather be independent of Spain entirely. Mexican and Cartagenan Republics had been declared and were issuing letters of marque.

In July 1816, Luis Aury, another Caribbean pirate, established a base on Galveston Island. He set up a town on the western end of the island, on the bay side of the island. He built an earth fort armed with a dozen cannon. He was condemning prizes in a "court of justice" he established and shipping goods to New Orleans to sell.

The Central Spanish government had largely suppressed Mexico's first independence movement by 1813, but remnants remained in Mexico's outlying territories, including Texas. The Mexican revolutionaries heard of Aury's pirate settlement and decided to use it. They appointed Aury as Galveston Island's governor, allowing Aury to organize an admiralty court to condemn prizes taken to Galveston. Aury accepted the position. It legitimized his piracy.

The worried Spanish decided to infiltrate the colony with a spy. Lafitte had been a Spanish spy. (The money was good.) He had been scouting the Mississippi basin for Spain. Luis Onis, Spain's minister to the United States, also ran Spain's intelligence services in North America. He told the Lafittes to find out what was going on in Galveston and to get Aury and the pirates to leave Galveston.

The brothers were soon sniffing out Galveston. Jean arrived in early April 1817 and swore allegiance to Aury's "Mexican" government. A few days later, Aury departed Galveston, carrying a Mexican invasion force to Soto la Marina in Tamaulipas. While Aury was gone, Lafitte took charge of the Mexican government in Galveston. He then returned to New Orleans to help Spain plan a scheme to capture Aury and remove his pirates from Galveston Island. Pierre and Jean returned to Galveston in May, supposedly to "help" Spain retake the island.

The brothers realized the possibilities Galveston offered. It was close to the United States, offering a market for any cargos captured. Unlike most of the Texas coast, Galveston offered sheltered anchorages inside the barrier island at either end of the island. They offered protection from Gulf storms and from invasion. (The entrances could be guarded by forts.) There was lots of Spanish shipping to be captured; using Mexico legitimized any seizures.

The best part? Spain would bankroll the enterprise since the brothers were conducting their operations under the guise of removing the pirates from Galveston.

The brothers proceeded to take over Galveston. During Aury's absence, they persuaded the men left on Galveston to accept Jean as their leader. By July, Aury realized he had been outmaneuvered. He took the men still loyal to him to Amelia Island in Florida, never to return to Galveston.

The brothers began running another piracy shell game. They used the collapsing Mexican insurrectionaries to legitimize their privateering. They used their connection with Spain and their supposed efforts to remove the pirates from Galveston to keep Spain (and to a lesser extent the United States) from removing them from Galveston. They used the pirates as cover for their real purpose in Galveston: smuggling.

Their real money came from smuggling slaves into the United States. The U.S. government barred importation of slaves into the United States after 1808. However, the porous and ill-defined border between Spain and the United States offered a mechanism to move African slaves profitably into the United States. The federal government paid a reward for information leading to the capture of illegal slaves. Informants received half the value the government got when it sold contraband slaves at auction. Lafitte became an informant, sometimes informing on slaves he smuggled into the United States. He did not collect as much profit as if he had sold them, but the earnings were legal and could not be seized. He used the U.S. government to launder his gains.

For a few years, the brothers lived large. Jean relocated the settlement, which he named Campeche, to the east end of the island, near the modern harbor. It was a better location for a harbor. He built a fort to protect his anchorage and he and his followers threw up a town. Jean even built a large, two-story frame house. It was painted red (probably barn red, made from iron oxide and linseed oil and commonly used on ships) and became known as Maison Rouge—or the Red House. He maintained a mistress there, reportedly "mulatto" and possibly a slave, and hosted visitors in high style.

Visitors and associates included many well-known individuals from early Texas history. They included James Long and wife Jane Wilkinson Long and Jim and Rezin Bowie. Baron Charles François Antoine Lallemand stopped at the Maison Rouge while trying to set up a Bourbon émigré colony in East Texas, as did George Graham. Graham had been sent by the U.S. government to investigate conditions in Texas. He visited Maison Rouge in August 1818.

Graham arrived at Lafitte's apogee. A month later, on September 9, a hurricane hit Galveston, flooded Campeche and sank Lafitte's ship. The

A Texas State Historical Marker shows where Jean Lafitte's Maison Rouge once stood on Galveston Island. The ruins behind the marker are those of a late-nineteenth-century mansion unconnected to Lafitte but add an appropriate touch of drama to the site. *Author photograph.*

Long Expedition and the French émigrés had brought unwanted attention to Lafitte's smuggling kingdom. The United States finally settled its border with Spain, and Spain had finally crushed the Mexican insurgents. Both nations wanted the pirates gone. Everyone was tired of Lafitte's argument that he was trying to wind down the colony. Spain withdrew support for Lafitte, finally realizing he was playing his own game and not supporting them.

In 1820, the U.S. Navy arrived in force to evict the Lafittes. He stalled the navy for a few months before bowing to the inevitable and relocating to Isla Mujeres off the coast of the Yucatan. Jean departed Galveston for the last time in May 1820, dismantling the fort and burning Maison Rouge and the buildings of Campeche as he left. Left behind were the ruins of his settlement and a lot of legends.

Lafitte probably died in 1825, somewhere on the South American mainland. Yet his ghost haunts Galveston as surely as if he had died there. Rumors of Lafitte treasure buried at the site of Maison Rouge continue to the present. Today, the site is surrounded by a chain-link fence to discourage treasure hunters. (Why Jean Lafitte would bury his fortune before making an orderly departure is a question no treasure hunter can adequately answer. Lafitte, a good businessman, would have placed his loot—properly laundered—in a bank to gain interest.) As the saying goes, when the legend becomes fact, print the legend.

5

THE TEXAS NAVY'S
FORGOTTEN FIRST STEAMSHIP

One ghost haunting the Texas coast is the Texas Navy. It is largely forgotten today, except for by history buffs. Its fans organized and maintain the Third Texas Navy to keep its memory alive and gain the privilege of addressing themselves as "admiral." (There may be as many honorary Texas Navy admirals as there are honorary Kentucky colonels.) Yet the Texas Navy is worth remembering. The first Texas Navy kept the Mexicans from reversing the victory at San Jacinto and crushing the Texas Revolution. The second Texas Navy prevented a Mexican invasion of the Republic of Texas in 1842 and 1843, allowing Texas to remain independent long enough to join the United States.

The first Texas Navy was a ragtag collection of sloops and schooners hastily purchased on the eve of the War of Texas Independence, armed, commissioned as warships by Texas's revolutionary congress and sent to guard the Texas coast from the Mexican navy. It wasn't much of a navy. It had only four warships, none over 125 tons or a crew larger than ninety men.

It was big enough, however. It helped gain Texas independence by keeping Mexican supplies from reaching the army of Mexican general (and president) Antonio López de Santa Anna. You can march an army from Mexico to Texas, but in 1836, you could not bring the food to feed it or the ammunition to replace what was expended in combat except by sea.

After the battle of San Jacinto, more than five thousand Mexican troops remained in Texas. The Texians, having defeated Santa Anna, thought they had won. Their army, except for a company of Texas Rangers, all went

A model of Zavala, Texas's first and only steam warship. This model was commissioned by Clive Cussler after his search for the ship in 1986. *Courtesy Clive Cussler.*

home. The Mexican government ordered their remaining units in Texas to continue the fight. The Texas Navy kept all but three supply ships from reaching the Texas coast and that company of Texas Rangers captured those three in Matagorda Bay. The Mexican troops had enough food to get back home but not enough to fight for a few more weeks and then go home if they lost again. Their generals decided discretion was indeed the better part of valor. They marched home.

Despite its contributions to winning Texas independence, the first Texas Navy got little love from the new republic. Navies cost money, which was in short supply in the Republic of Texas. By October 1837, all four of its ships had been lost. One was seized in the United States and sold to pay off debts the Texas Navy accumulated. Two others were wrecked, and the Mexican navy captured one in a two-on-one battle.

Texas was still at war with Mexico. The Mexican government deposed Santa Anna after his capture at the Battle of San Jacinto, repudiating the peace treaty Santa Anna signed, granting Texas independence. Although the Mexican forces in Texas disregarded orders to continue the effort to put down the rebellion and returned home, Mexico never recognized Texas independence. It insisted that Texas remained part of Mexico as the state of Coahuila y Tejas and was in a state of insurrection.

Between 1837 and 1842, Mexico kept assembling armies to reconquer Texas. Fortunately for the republic, every time Mexico was ready to move, another Mexican state would rebel, declaring its independence. The invasion of Texas kept getting postponed to put down these new rebellions. Mexican armies could only reach Texas by crossing the vast expanse of the arid and sparsely El Norte states. Despite this, Mexico twice invaded Texas overland in 1842. Predictably, Mexico could not supply those armies, which were forced to withdraw.

However, Texas remained vulnerable to an invasion of its seacoast. In the 1830s and 1840s, before the railroad and automobile, oceans and rivers were the main highways of commerce. Mexico might have found it hard to supply an army in Texas overland, but moving supplies across the Gulf of Mexico was easy. They could even pack ships with troops and take them to the Texas coast. The Republic of Texas had no standing army. Militia took time to assemble (and was not that effective anyway). Mexico could have conquered Texas with a seaborne invasion. The first Texas Navy guarded Texas's maritime frontier through the end of 1837 but lost its last ship in October 1837.

The Texas Congress became concerned about its undefended coast. On November 4, 1837, it passed a naval appropriations act authorizing a new and sizable navy. It was the birth of the second Texas Navy.

This time, Texas decided to do it right. The Texas Congress envisioned a new navy, one not made up of merchant vessels hastily converted to warships. Instead, the Texas Navy was to get six ships, new construction, designed and built as warships: a full-rigged sloop-of-war, two brigs-of-war, and three armed schooners.

This was a formidable force. The sloop-of-war could beat any three brigs in the Mexican navy. The two brigs-of-war were significantly larger than their Mexican counterparts, twice as large as most of the Mexican navy's brigs. The three schooners were dispatch vessels, used for scouting and to carry messages.

The appropriations bill authorized purchase of an additional warship, one unlike anything in the Texas Navy, the Mexican navy or most of the other world's navies: a steam-powered warship. It was named *Zavala* for the Lorenzo de Zavala, a Tejano who served as the first vice-president of the Republic of Texas but had died of pneumonia in November 1836.

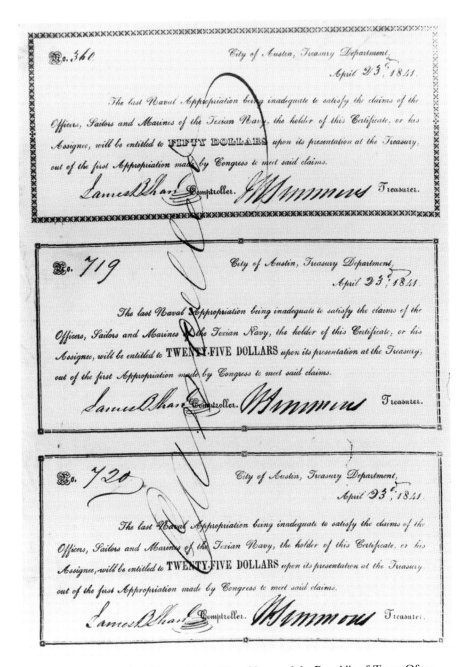

Money was a perpetual problem with the Texas Navy and the Republic of Texas. Often, Texas Navy officers and men were paid in notes such as these, which had to be redeemed in Austin rather than at the ports where *Zavala* docked. *USNHHC.*

Zavala did not start out as a warship. Built in 1836 by John Vaughan and Son of Philadelphia, it was designed as a passenger-carrying steam packet. First known as *Charleston*, it serviced the Charleston–Philadelphia route from its 1836 launch until November 1838, when the Texas Navy purchased it. It was 201 feet long, with a 24-foot beam and a 12-foot depth of hold. It probably displaced between 950 and 1,000 tons, had a carrying capacity of 569 tons and could accommodate 120 passengers on the three-day voyage between the two ports. The Texas navy commissioned it on March 23, 1839.

The decision to purchase a steamship and outfit it as an armed warship had to be both surprising and controversial.

Steamships were in general use by the late 1830s. River-faring steamboats were common. They plied inland and coastal North American waterways as far west as Texas. Oceangoing steamers were a little rarer, but they were being used especially as passenger packets along the U.S. Atlantic and Gulf Coasts.

There were two big problems with using steamships as warships. The first was that the low-efficiency steam plants of the 1830s ate fuel. No ship could carry enough fuel, even coal with its high energy density, to use steam to cross long distances. The steam plant was used only during periods of calm or when the wind was blowing in the wrong direction. It was especially useful for entering and exiting harbors—or to maneuver during battle—but all oceangoing steamships of the period depended on sail for most of their cruising.

Steam warships had another drawback. In battle, they were extremely vulnerable to combat damage. Although on larger ships, boilers were typically in the hull, their steam drums and the engines they powered were above the waterline, exposed to shot and shell. Worse, steamers of the era depended on paddlewheels for propulsion. The paddle boxes were large and located just aft of amidships. A single round shot, even from a relatively small gun, could destroy the paddlewheel, immobilizing the ship.

The result was that in 1838 there were relatively few steam warships. Great Britain's Royal Navy had the most with fifty-five. Most were tugs to move ships in and out of harbor. France came in second at thirty-seven. Most other nations could number the steamships in their navies on their fingers, the majority requiring only one hand to complete the count. The United States Navy then had but one steam warship, USS *Fulton*, which had entered service the year before. Mexico had none.

Zavala used two horizontal single-expansion, reciprocating, low-pressure walking beam steam engines powered by the steam generated by two boilers. The steam engine pistons used a walking beam to drive the ship's paddlewheels. Coal was the preferred fuel, although if coal was unavailable, its boilers could be fired with cordwood or even wooden furniture and fittings. It could cruise at nine knots under combined steam and sail.

Conversion of *Zavala* into a warship initially consisted of adding five guns to the vessel, one long nine-pounder on a pivot mount and four medium twelve-pounders on carriages, two on each broadside. (Tom Henderson Wells, in *Commodore Moore and the Texas Navy* stated *Zavala* carried four broadside medium eighteen-pounders and a long eighteen-pounder and a long twelve-pounder on pivot mounts.) That was it. It went through further alterations after leaving Charleston and arriving at New Orleans. There, its passenger ship fittings were removed and sold.

Zavala would have a short but memorable career in the Texas Navy. Having spent nearly the equivalent of $300,000 (U.S. dollars) to buy outfit and man the Texas Navy's new ships, a new Texas congress, elected in 1840, decided spending $5,000 a month to maintain it was excessive. The Pastry War, fought between France and Mexico in 1838–39, contributed to the legislature's belief that the navy was an unnecessary expense, The French swept Mexico from the seas. By March 1839, Mexico was temporarily without a navy. The *Zavala* was a particular problem in the legislature's

Maintaining *Zavala* proved challenging for the Texas Navy. In addition to the perpetual shortage of money to pay for maintenance and repair, Galveston in the 1840s was a frontier town with few facilities for working on steam engines. *USNHHC.*

view. It took expensive engineers and machine shops to maintain its engines. Both were in short supply on the Gulf Coast in the United States and were virtually impossible to find in Texas.

Commodore Edwin Moore, commanding the Texas Navy, talked the congress out of mothballing the Texas Navy. He was convinced the navy was not only necessary but could also pay for itself through prizes captured. Back then, warships could capture ships of a nation with which they were at war and sell the captured ship as a prize for its value. Part of the value went to the crew, the rest to the navy. Since Mexico was at war with Texas, Texas could capture Mexican ships and sell them in the United States for hard cash. Moore was able to gain a stay of execution for most of the Texas Navy's ships, including the *Zavala*.

Zavala soon proved its worth at the navy's home port of Galveston. It could tow Texas Navy ships in and out of that port, something frequently needed. This saved the expense of hiring steam tugs. Soon, *Zavala*, two schooners and the sloop-of-war *Austin* were patrolling the waters around Mexico's major seaport, Veracruz. Unfortunately, the Republic of Texas's perpetual poverty kept *Zavala* short of rations for its men and fuel for its engines.

Things got more desperate after *Zavala* was damaged in a storm in October 1840. It had been anchored off the Tabasco River to collect firewood when its anchors dragged. It was saved only through the superior seamanship and ingenuity of its captain. But money was needed to repair it.

In 1840, Mexico was undergoing one of its periodic civil wars, the Federalist Revolution of 1839–41. One faction, bankrolled by France, was led by General Juan Pablo Anaya. They needed to capture the town of San Juan Bautista eighty miles up the Tabasco River. He had only 125 troops available. His Centralist opponents had 600 holding the town. Although technically at war with Texas, Anaya made common cause with Moore and the Texas Navy. He offered the Texians $25,000 if the Texas Navy helped him capture San Juan Bautista.

It required getting *Austin*, one of the schooners and an armed brig controlled by Yucatan rebels up the Tabasco River to turn their guns on the town. The river was deep and wide enough to hold the ships but too narrow to sail up. *Zavala* towed the three ships up the river. Once they arrived, the ships awed the Centralist garrison into surrender. Anaya paid $10,000 up front and the rest within thirty days.

That and several captured prizes should have paid the expenses for the Texas Navy, including a badly needed refit for *Zavala*. Instead, following Britain's recognition of Texas as an independent nation, the republic's

Zavala's boiler after being recovered from the bottom of Galveston's harbor in 2015. It and the other surviving artifacts of *Zavala* are located at the Texas Maritime Museum in Rockport, Texas. *Courtesy of the Conservation Research Laboratory at Texas A&M University.*

government convinced itself recognition by Mexico and peace would soon follow. Most of the Texas Navy, including *Zavala*, was laid up at Galveston in early 1841.

Zavala ended its days in Galveston. There was talk of selling it, but it remained just talk. Various attempts were made to bring the ship back to active service in 1841 and 1842. To do so required an expensive overhaul of *Zavala*'s steam engines and boilers. The penny-pinching republic refused to pay for it. By June 1842, the badly leaking *Zavala* was run ashore to keep it from sinking. A year later, it was stricken from the Texas Navy. Everything still useful was stripped and sold. The hull was allowed to sink into the mud of Galveston's harbor. Zavala remains sank into mud that was once part of the harbor but filled in as the island was expanded in the late nineteenth and early twentieth centuries.

The ship was gone, but its memory lingered on. In 1986, author Clive Cussler financed an expedition to locate the ship's remains. Cussler's National Underwater Marine Agency, in concert with the Texas Antiquities Commission, eventually found what was believed to be its remains under a parking lot near the grain elevator in Galveston's port area. Cussler commissioned two models of Zavala—one he kept and one he presented to the State of Texas. Then, in 2015, with a planned expansion of cruise ship terminal scheduled for the lot, a second excavation occurred at the site. Zavala's remains, including much of its steam plant, were excavated from their location near Pier 30 and conserved. Today, they reside in the Texas Maritime Museum in Rockport, Texas.

6

WOODEN SHIPS AND SAIL BEAT IRON STEAMSHIPS

Wooden sailing ships firing solid shot cannot beat steamships, especially iron-hulled steamships firing guns armed with explosive shells. This has been an axiom ever since the 1853 Battle of Sinope. Sinope was a Turkish port on the Black Sea. On November 30, 1853, a Russian fleet that included three steamships went into Sinope's harbor and systematically destroyed a Turkish fleet there. The Russian fleet was much larger than the Turkish fleet, both sides had wooden ships and steamships played a minor part in the battle.

The difference was that the Russians had explosive shells while the Turks did not. The battle showed the superiority of shot and steam, and navies began replacing pure sailing ships firing solid shot with steam-powered warships carrying shell-firing guns. However, within a decade of the Battle of Sinope, navies around the world were building iron-armored steamships. The Royal Navy's 1861 *Warrior* and the battle between CSS *Virginia* and USS *Monitor* in Hampton Roads brought down the curtain on the age of fighting sail.

During the transition from wood and sail to iron and steam, several battles were fought between wooden sailing warships and iron-hulled steam-powered warships. The side with the steam-powered iron ships won almost every battle. There was only one battle where wooden sailing ships triumphed. Almost inevitably, in a victory as improbable as this one, Texas—and the Texas Navy—was involved. Almost equally inevitably, the Texas Navy won.

Edwin Moore left the United States Navy as a lieutenant to become the commodore and senior officer in the Texas Navy. He led the Texas Navy and was commanded the flagship at the Battle of Campeche. *USNHHC.*

In 1838, the Texas legislature transformed the Texas Navy from nonexistent to a regional powerhouse. In 1840, the Texas Navy was at the peak of its strength, with the three schooners, two brigs, a full-rigged sloop-of-war and an armed steamship. The sailing warships were the latest in naval architecture. Designed in Baltimore, then a leading center for naval architecture, they provided Texas with a balanced force that could operate both in coastal waters and on the high seas. All were shallow-draft so they could enter Galveston Harbor. The ships were armed with primarily Columbiads, medium-ranged cannons capable of firing explosive shells. With Mexico's navy in possession of France following Mexico's defeat in the Pastry War of 1838–39, Texas ruled the Gulf of Mexico.

Unfortunately, the tide went out on the Texas Navy almost as soon as it reached its flood. Moore arrived at Galveston in January 1840. He spent a frustrating eighteen months battling a Republic Congress intent on eliminating the Texas Navy as a cost-cutting measure as much as he spent fighting the Mexican armed forces. By September 1841, the schooner *San Antonio* had been wrecked, and the rest of the navy was worn out, requiring repair. *Zavala* was unseaworthy.

Britain negotiated a six-month truce between Mexico and Texas. The Texas Congress, anxious for a return to normality, misinterpreted the truce as a de facto peace. Texas laid up the fleet to save money. In 1841, the Texas Navy, except for the *San Antonio* surveying the Texas coast, and the *San Bernard*, running diplomatic errands, was rotting in Galveston. Even *Austin* was in reduced condition for harbor duty.

In reality, Mexico was again planning to retake its breakaway province. The Mexican Centralist government, led by Anastasio Bustamante, had been replaced by a more militant regime, headed by Santa Anna, the victor at the Alamo and the loser at San Jacinto. In June, the truce collapsed.

Mirabeau Lamar, then president of the Republic of Texas, authorized an expedition against Santa Fe, then part of Mexico. Moore had earlier formed an informal alliance with the Mexican Federalist faction in the Yucatan. Lamar began negotiating an alliance with these Yucateco forces. The Yucatan rebellion started as an effort to restore the 1824 Mexican constitution. Its leaders controlled their region but could not extend control over the entire country. Instead, the Yucatecos declared independence.

Without Yucatan's ports, ships and seamen, Mexico's reconquest of Texas was impossible. The Yucatan Republic lacked an effective fleet in 1841. Texas had a navy but lacked the resources to use it. Lamar decided to solve the problems of both Texas and the Yucatan by combining them. He offered to lease the Texas Navy to the Yucatan.

On September 17, 1841, two republics signed an alliance. The agreement obligated Texas to support the Yucatan with three warships and the Yucatan to pay Texas $8,000 per month as long as at least three Texas warships were available. The Yucatan even offered to refit the steamship *Zavala* at their expense if it was included in the expedition.

On October 13, Moore received orders to sail with three ships but to keep the cost below $8,000 per month. It took Moore two months to clear the Galveston bar with *Austin*, *San Antonio* and *San Bernard*. He sailed on December 13, the day Lamar's term as president of the Texas Republic ended. At sea, Moore opened sealed orders directing him to sail to Sisal and support the Yucatan Republic.

Sam Houston replaced Lamar. On December 15, Houston sent orders to Galveston, recalling Moore. The orders were forwarded via a pilot boat that proved unable to find the Texas Navy. Houston later grumbled that the boat had been misled due to "peculiar influences in Galveston."

Moore arrived at Sisal on January 6. Instead of an ally's welcome, he discovered that the Yucatan was expecting peace with Mexico. Since the

Austin, the Texas Navy flagship was ship-rigged wooden sailing sloop-of-war. It had one gun deck and was armed with muzzle-loading smoothbore guns known as Columbaids, which could fire shells as well as solid shot. This model provides a best guess on its probable appearance. *Model and photograph by Charlie Cozewith.*

peace treaty was not finalized, Moore negotiated a compromise with the Yucatecos. The Yucatan agreed to pay the Texas Navy, which would operate out of Sisal, but suspended joint operations pending resolution of negotiations. *Austin* and *San Bernard* blockaded the Mexican coast, while the *San Antonio* returned to Galveston for orders.

Word trickled back in February that the Santa Fe expedition had ended with the entire Texian army captured. Mexico rejected the treaty negotiated with the Yucatan and invaded Texas in March 1842, briefly occupying San Antonio.

When Moore learned about the raid into San Antonio—and that an army of thirty thousand was massing against the Yucatan—he took the offensive. Seizing several Mexican merchant ships, he challenged the Mexican Navy, demonstrating off Veracruz. Moore hoped to lure the Mexicans into battle before all of their reinforcements arrived, but the Mexican navy played a waiting game.

It worked. Texian disorganization proved deadlier to the Texas Navy than the Mexican ships. The *San Antonio* mutinied in New Orleans in February, due to discontent fueled by poor food and absent pay. In late March, Moore was sent the brig *Wharton* and orders to blockade the Mexican coast but no additional supplies or money.

Short on supplies, Moore returned to Texas in April. In May, the entire officer corps, frustrated at being ignored by the government, tendered resignations. They had not been paid in a year, a partial payment at that. Moore talked them into withdrawing the resignations through force of personality.

Moore spent the rest of 1842 struggling to prepare the Texas Navy for sea. He purchased a steamship from his own funds, renamed it *Merchant* and offered it to the Texas Navy as a replacement for the *Zavala*, which had sunk dockside. Year's end found the seaworthy portions of the Texas Navy outfitting in American ports.

The war continued. Mexico began receiving the new steam warships it had ordered. The first, the *Regenerador*, arrived in April 1842. It was a former merchant steamer, converted much in the same way as the *Zavala*. The others, the *Moctezuma* and *Guadaloupe*, arrived in the summer and fall. They were among the first ships built and designed as steam warships. Both were originally built with an eye toward selling them to the Royal Navy. The *Guadaloupe* was the first iron-hulled warship ever built and was built with watertight compartments. Both carried large, shell-firing cannon; were commanded by half-pay Royal Navy officers; and had mainly British crews.

Mexico captured three Yucateco warships in July and August. Carmen fell to the Mexicans on August 30. Mexico besieged Campeche with eight thousand soldiers. The Mexicans again raided San Antonio in September. That month, the schooner *San Antonio* disappeared while carrying dispatches to the Yucatan. It probably foundered in a hurricane. In October, *Merchant* ran aground and was lost.

Efforts against Mexico—both land and sea—seemed to progress in spite of Houston, rather than due to him. He called up the militia but refused to allow it to be used offensively. He ordered the navy back to Texas to be used as port guards. He blocked funds intended for the navy and army. He allowed a prize taken by the navy to return to Mexico, laden with gunpowder.

Some historians believe Houston was deliberately weakening Texas to force American or British intervention. Houston's motivations were more complex—he believed that Texas lacked funds to pursue an aggressive war, overestimated the effectiveness of militia, misunderstood maritime issues

The Mexican warship *Guadalupe* was an iron-hulled paddle steam warship. It had been built in Birkenhead, England, and purchased by the Mexican navy in 1842 as a response to the Texas Navy's *Zavala*. While iron-hulled, it was not armored. *AC.*

and trusted that his friendship with Santa Anna would prevent a second invasion in 1842.

In January 1843, Houston moved to abolish the Texas Navy. He pushed a bill through Congress, dissolving the navy despite reports that Mexico planned a naval invasion of Texas in the spring. Keeping the bill's passage a secret from the public and the navy, Houston sent commissioners to New Orleans to meet with Moore and sell the navy.

Moore instead convinced the naval commissioners to let him take the navy to Campeche to lift the siege. The Yucatan would pay the expenses, and the two ships in New Orleans, the *Austin* and the *Wharton*, were ready for sea, not the hulks the commissioners expected. The balance was tipped when another messenger arrived from the Yucatan with news that the Mexicans intended to sail to Texas once the Yucatan fell. Moore sailed on April 15.

Houston got wind of these plans. Angered, Houston issued a proclamation declaring Moore and his ships as pirates. Morgan, the naval commissioner who remained with Moore, declared the proclamation invalid.

When he arrived, Moore learned that the *Moctezuma* was escorting troopships to Telchac, where a Mexican army was moving on Merida, the Yucateco capitol. Campeche still held out, blockaded by the Mexican fleet, but its fall was expected soon. Moore heard that Mexico planned to re-embark the army once the Yucatan fell and land on the Texas Gulf coast. Hoping to ambush the *Moctezuma*, Moore sailed for Telchac on April 19.

He arrived the day after the *Moctezuma* departed. Moore pursued the ship west along the coast, lifting the Mexican blockade at Sisal along the way. Joined by remnants of the Yucateco navy, he continued until he found the Mexican fleet off Campeche on April 29.

The next morning, battle was joined. A desultory, long-range skirmish fought over five hours, it was the first battle where explosive shells were used. The Mexicans, determined to use their range advantage, never closed. The day ended with Moore holding the field. Mexico's real losses occurred before the battle, when the commander of *Moctezuma* died of yellow fever. The captain of the *Guadaloupe* wanted to avoid the same fate. He was already under pressure from the Royal Navy because he was serving in a foreign navy. Unwilling to risk his lifetime Royal Navy half-pay, he too resigned. The new commanders, Mexican nationals, lacked experience commanding steamships.

Over the next two weeks, Moore attempted to engage the Mexican fleet for two weeks. Each time Moore came out, Marín, the Mexican naval commander, backed away from Moore's ships, hoping to fight when the wind was calm and his opponents were immobilized. Santa Anna, frustrated by the delay, ordered Marín to attack. On May 16, Moore sailed out and met the Mexicans in combat.

The Battle of Campeche was a battle that saw both sides use shell to little effect. The Mexicans engaged at extreme range, depending on their steam plants and long-range guns to carry the day. *Austin* could only respond with a pair of long guns borrowed from the Yucatecos.

The Mexicans maintained their range because of the vulnerability of their paddle wheels to damage. Shell fusing in 1843 was so primitive that most shells exploded harmlessly at long ranges, negating its advantages. Moore could not close the range as long as the Mexican steam engines worked. They proved reliable, so Moore got few opportunities to damage their paddle boxes.

The battle was a bloody draw. The Mexican ships were crammed with troops. Any hit caused casualties. The Texian ships proved vulnerable to the few shells that actually struck. By the end of the day, both sides had used most of their ammunition. The Mexicans sailed home. Both sides claimed victory.

Who really won? Wooden sailing warships repelled a force with steamships. The Mexican navy failed to drive off the defenders, breaking the blockade

Austin with *Wharton* behind it is depicted in action against the Mexican navy off the Yucatan in 1843. *USNHHC.*

of Campeche. Campeche survived. The Yucatan Republic survived another year. The Mexican invasion of Texas was postponed.

As the Centralists withdrew from the Yucatan, rumors flew about Moore's status as a declared outlaw. The Yucatecos prevented Moore from destroying the Mexican fleet after June 14, even as the Mexican steamships swung unmanned at their moorings when their crews' enlistments expired. On June 29, the Texas Navy sailed from Campeche for Galveston. On arrival, the ships were laid up for the last time.

Houston dishonorably discharged Moore. Moore demanded a court-martial. At his 1844 trial, Moore was acquitted of eighteen charges. The remaining four were minor misdemeanors. Houston refused to return Moore's commission and thus matters stood until annexation.

The Yucatan Republic fell to the Centralists in 1845. That year, the United States annexed Texas, triggering the Mexican-American War. The four surviving Texas Navy ships were absorbed into the United States Navy. None sailed again. Texas Navy officers were blocked entry into the United States Navy, although eventually, they received back pay and pensions for their Texas service.

Moore left Texas, settled in New York, became an inventor and died there in 1865. Texas rewarded him by naming a county for him. Given the obscurity that cloaked the Texas Navy, it seems appropriate that Moore County is in the Texas Panhandle—far from the Gulf where Moore changed history.

7

THE FATE OF THE *HATTERAS*

The Union navy ruled the seven seas and most of the Gulf of Mexico during the American Civil War. But weird things happened when the Union crossed west of the Sabine River, the border dividing Louisiana from Texas. Then things went wrong. Not always but generally at the worst possible moment. During the Civil War the U.S. Navy lost four battles with Confederate naval forces. One was the famous battle in Hampton Roads where CSS *Virginia* (née *Merrimack*) sank the wooden frigate *Congress* and forced *Cumberland* aground the day before USS *Monitor* arrived to fight the first battle between ironclads. The other three were fought off the Texas coast.

The Union lost scads of merchantmen to Confederate raiders, but those were unarmed civilian ships, not warships. The Union navy fought battles that ended indecisively, with the Union failing to achieve its objective, such as the bombardment of Fort Sumter by Union ironclads in 1863. While the Union failed to force the fort's surrender, that is a far cry from losing a warship to the enemy. After 1862, the Union navy only suffered those kinds of losses off Texas's coast.

One humiliating loss occurred off the Texas coast, just over the horizon from Galveston, the loss of the gunboat *Hatteras* at the hands of the Confederate raider *Alabama*. The loss was bitter because it was unnecessary, the result of carelessness on the part of the Union commander. It was made worse because the North muffed an easy opportunity to destroy the Confederacy's deadliest commerce raider early in its career. It came hard on another early U.S. Navy defeat at the hands of the rebellious Texans. These

SURPRISE AND CAPTURE OF THE UNITED STATES STEAMER "HARRIET LANE," BY THE CONFEDERATES, UNDER GENERAL MAGRUDER, AND THE DESTRUCTION OF THE FLAGSHIP "WESTFIELD" IN GALVESTON HARBOR, TEXAS, JANUARY 1st, 1863.

The Naval Battle of Galveston, fought on New Year's Eve 1862 and into the morning hours of January 1, 1863, set in train a series of events that led to the United States Navy's only defeat on the high seas during the Civil War. *USNHHC.*

battles haunted the North for the rest of the war, and its ghosts still linger off the Texas coast.

The Union fought a pretty good war against Texas through the end of 1862. In October 1862, they captured Galveston, the only seaport on the Texas coast with a sheltered harbor. Virtually every other port on the Texas coast was then open roadsteads, exposing ships to tropical cyclones and seasonal gales. Galveston's capture shut down the best Texas port from which the Confederates could run the Union blockade.

About the time the Union got Galveston, Texas got Confederate general John Magruder. He was known as "Prince John" due to his courtly manner and interests in theatrics, which he occasionally used on the battlefield to confound his enemies. Magruder had gotten crosswise with General Robert E. Lee during the Seven Days Battle earlier that year. When Lee reorganized the Army of Northern Virginia, Lee left Magruder, whom Lee believed incompetent, without a command.

Magruder was made commander of the District of Texas, New Mexico and Arizona. It was a consolation prize that moved him as far beyond the Mississippi River as you could get and still be in the Confederacy. At Malvern Hill, Magruder had been unlucky and cursed by bad orders. Yet Magruder was actually highly competent and soon proved both competence and aggressiveness on the Texas coast.

Magruder immediately began planning to retake Galveston. On January 31, 1862, he launched a midnight combined arms assault. Texas troops stormed across the Galveston causeway, attacking the Union soldiers garrisoning Galveston. A fleet of armed Confederate steamboats simultaneously attacked the Union flotilla in Galveston's harbor. The Confederate steamboats were called "cottonclads" because they were armored with cotton bales capable of stopping small arms and shrapnel. By dawn on New Year's Day, the Union troops were preparing to surrender; one Union warship, *Harriet Lane*, had been captured; and the Union flagship *Westfield* had been destroyed to prevent capture. One Confederate warship had been sunk, but the Confederates soon refloated it off the harbor's shallow bottom and repaired it.

The surviving Yankee ships scuttled back to New Orleans, where they reported the loss of Galveston to their commander, Admiral David Farragut, and to the commander of the Union's Army of the Gulf, General Nathaniel Banks.

Banks was one of the truly wretched Union generals, so inept the Confederates nicknamed him "Commissary Banks" for his performance during the 1862 Shenandoah Campaign. Banks was outmaneuvered and outfought. Worse, his inept performance allowed Stonewall Jackson's troops to capture Banks's supply depot, a mountain of stores that allowed the starving Confederate army to continue the campaign.

But Banks was too politically connected to simply discharge after this performance. Instead, Lincoln shipped him someplace where it was hoped that Banks would do less damage: New Orleans. There, any damage caused by his ineptitude would at least occur in a theater far from the decisive ones in the upper Mississippi basin and the East. One reason the Confederates retook Galveston was that Banks had procrastinated sending reinforcements. Had those troops arrived in mid-December instead of waiting until mid-January, the Union garrison would have been too strong to have been beaten and could have held out until the Union navy returned in force to relieve them.

Farragut never procrastinated. He immediately dispatched his flag captain, Henry H. Bell, with the first-class sloop-of-war *Brooklyn* and gunboats *Cayuga*,

CSS *Alabama* was a raider built in Britain for the Confederacy. Rumors of Union reinforcements sent to Galveston led *Alabama*'s captain to go there in hopes of finding Union soldiers still aboard the troopships carrying them. *AC.*

New London, Hatteras and *Sciota* to Galveston to investigate the situation. Bell had orders to collect *Clifton* and *Sachem* along the way. Could the Union retake Galveston with a quick counterattack? Farragut wanted to try.

Also in the Gulf at this time was the Confederate raider CSS *Alabama.* Originally launched as No. 290 at Birkenhead Iron Works, it was launched on May 14, 1862, at Liverpool, England. Designed and built as a commerce raider, its construction violated British law. As *Hull 290*, it managed to slip out of Liverpool just before the British authorities could seize it. It reached the Azores in August, was armed, named *Alabama* and commissioned a Confederate warship on August 24, 1862. Since then, it had been capturing and burning U.S.-flagged merchant ships in the Atlantic. In November 1862, it began a raid into the Gulf of Mexico.

Alabama was taking a Christmas break at the Areas Keys. While there, Raphael Semmes, *Alabama*'s captain, got word of Banks sending troops to Galveston and that they were due to arrive around January 10. The "word" was garbled. Semmes assumed this was an invasion force rather than reinforcements. An invasion force would have to anchor outside Galveston Harbor in an open roadstead. Semmes decided that it was worth risking *Alabama* to destroy a Union invasion fleet. He planned to steam into the transports and sink as many as he could before the escorting Yankee warships stopped him. Semmes believed *Alabama* could sink at least a dozen transports before any escorts could interfere. He might sink even more if he concentrated on the transports, even at the risk of losing *Alabama*.

Semmes's plan was obsolete before he arrived. The Confederates had retaken Galveston, and Banks had cancelled the troop convoy. Late afternoon on January 11, 1863, found CSS *Alabama* off the Texas Gulf coast thirty miles southeast of Galveston Island. Instead of finding a fleet of transports, his lookouts spotted Bell's squadron of warships. The Union ships had spent the previous day bombarding Galveston and most of the 11th trying to decide what to do next.

Semmes hauled up to assess the situation. While the enemy squadron was hull down, their masts clearly showed that they were warships. His lookouts counted five ships. (They may have missed two that were inshore or Bell may have detached his other two vessels.) Semmes had no intention of battling five warships no matter how badly he wanted a fight. *Alabama* had no chance against that many enemy warships. Yet Semmes was reluctant to simply leave. Then he saw an opportunity. One ship was leaving the squadron and coming toward *Alabama*.

Bell's lookouts spotted *Alabama*'s masts. Bell detached one of his ships to investigate the strange sail. Unaware that *Alabama* was in the Gulf of Mexico and preoccupied with Galveston, Bell spent too little time considering the implications of that sighting. He assumed the ship possibly a blockade runner using the opportunity to visit a Galveston under new ownership. The only Confederate warships in the area that Bell knew of were Confederate cottonclads, converted riverboats lacking the masts of the unidentified ship. Bell sent *Hatteras* to investigate. Had Bell gone himself, in the flagship *Brooklyn*, he possibly could have become the man that sank the *Alabama*.

Hatteras was an iron-hulled sidewheel gunboat. Originally *St. Mary*, a civilian steamer, the navy purchased it during its 1861 expansion. Its five-gun armament, one twenty-pound Parrott rifle on a pivot mount and four short thirty-two-pound smoothbores on broadside mounts, was adequate against its usual foes, blockade runners or cottonclads armed with a thirty-two-pounder or two. It was not enough to face *Alabama*. The Confederate raider carried one seven-inch, one-hundred-pound Blakely Rifle; one eight-inch, sixty-eight-pound Blakely Smoothbore; and six long thirty-two-pound smoothbore cannon.

Semmes switched *Alabama* from sail to steam power. He brought his boilers up to pressure and engaged his engine, slowly steaming east, away from the

HOMER C. BLAKE.

When Captain Henry Bell's lookouts spotted a strange ship approaching Galveston, Bell sent *Hatteras*, skippered by Lieutenant Commander Homer C. Blake (*shown*) to investigate. Blake was cautious, but he sailed into a trap. *AC.*

Yankee squadron. Semmes kept his speed low to allow his pursuer to draw near. As they gradually increased the distance from the Union squadron, Semmes recognized the oncoming ship as a gunboat, a purchased merchantman converted to a warship, not a purpose-built man-of-war. He would have known the unknown gunboat would have a broadside weight of metal smaller than his own.

Lieutenant Commander Homer C. Blake, a competent and experienced officer, commanded *Hatteras*. A regular officer, his United States Navy career began in 1840. He soon recognized the strange sail was a steamer with the appearance of a warship. *Hatteras* should have been slower than the strange ship it was overhauling. Blake suspected he was being lured away from the Union squadron. He signaled his suspicions to *Brooklyn*. Either the signal was missed as dusk approached or it was ignored. Blake cleared *Hatteras* for action and continued the chase alone.

By the time *Hatteras* came within hail of *Alabama*, it was dark. *Hatteras* was over twenty miles from the other Union warships, enough distance that the two groups of ships could not see each other in the darkness. Blake hailed and asked the strange ship's identity. Semmes replied that it was an English warship. Blake later reported that he was told the ship was HMS *Vixen*. A master's mate aboard *Hatteras* later told Bell that the ship claimed to be HMS *Spitfire*. In his memoirs, Semmes stated that he called it HMS *Petrel*. Regardless, everyone agreed *Alabama* was pretending to be British, consistent with its country of origin. Blake identified his ship, revealing to Semmes that he had caught a lone United States Navy warship.

Blake was unconvinced the other ship was British. Suspicious, he told Semmes that *Hatteras* was sending a boat to examine the ship. Semmes waited until *Hatteras*'s boat was in the water. Then he identified his ship as CSS *Alabama* and opened fire. Almost instantly, *Hatteras* returned fire. *Hatteras*'s boat with six sailors and a master's mate aboard was caught between the exchange of gunfire. They rowed out of the way, remaining spectators through the rest of the fight.

It was a short-range battle. The ships were separated by no more than fifty to one hundred yards. *Hatteras* fired rapidly, hoping to attract the attention of the nearby squadron through the volume of gunfire. Flashes of gunfire could be seen from Galveston rooftops during the fight. Bell and his squadron heard the gunfire but were fogbound, unable to move until dawn.

Meanwhile, *Alabama* fired deliberately, using its larger guns to deadly effect. While *Hatteras* was iron-hulled, it was not armored. Its plating shattered when struck by *Alabama*'s shot. Shells penetrated the hold and landed amidships in the wardroom. They struck the engine, disabling it. It was impossible to run the fire pumps or move *Hatteras*. After just twelve minutes, *Hatteras* was burning and sinking. *Alabama* was almost completely undamaged. Blake recognized further resistance was pointless. He flooded his magazine to keep it from exploding. To indicate that he had struck, Blake fired a gun on the unengaged side and hoisted a light on *Hatteras*.

Semmes steamed over, asking if *Hatteras* had surrendered. Blake replied that it had. Semmes offered assistance. Once told *Hatteras* was sinking, Semmes took *Hatteras*'s crew aboard *Alabama*. Soon after being evacuated, *Hatteras* settled to the shallow Gulf bottom. By then, *Alabama* had doused its lights, hoisted sail and was departing the area.

In a battle lasting fewer than fifteen minutes, *Alabama* destroyed *Hatteras*, leaving it in a sinking condition. Blake and most of this crew were taken prisoner. *USNHHC.*

At 7:30 p.m., Bell sent *Brooklyn*, *Sciota* and *Cayuga* in search of *Hatteras*. *Brooklyn*, with Bell aboard, steamed the direction of the gun flashes seen the previous night, while *Sciota* and *Cayuga* searched east and west of *Brooklyn*. *Brooklyn* soon reached the site of the battle, where it was greeted by *Hatteras*'s masts. The sea was less than sixty feet deep. The mastheads were awash, with the topmasts sticking up from the water. Other debris was visible, including *Hatteras*'s wooden hurricane deck, which had floated free.

The next day, searchers found the *Hatteras*'s boat with its seven-man crew. They gave the first account of the battle from Union eyes. Further reports followed after Semmes released Blake, his officers and his men at neutral Jamaica. *Alabama* would continue marauding for another eighteen months, until USS *Kearsarge* ran it to ground off Cherbourg, France.

Although Bell suggested *Hatteras* could be refloated from the shallow waters of what is now called Flower Garden Banks. It never was. It remains on Flower Garden Banks, its hull largely settled three feet below the seabed. It could be said to haunt the U.S. Navy. It was the only warship sunk on open waters by a Confederate warship during the Civil War.

The wreck is now in the National Register of Historic Places and is a popular dive destination. If you visit, don't take anything from the ship as a souvenir. It remains the property of the U.S. Navy, which will haunt you if you do and they discover it.

8

SHIPWRECK AT A MUD FORT (THE BATTLE OF SABINE PASS)

It may have been the Civil War's most improbable victory. Forty-one Irishmen manning six cast-off cannon mounted in a mud fort repelled an invasion force of five warships, twenty-two transports, over fifty cannon and over five thousand men. The victorious leader's name—Dick Dowling—seems perfect for a boy's thriller. The battle changed the Civil War in Texas, keeping Texas free from Union occupation until Major General Gordon Granger landed at Galveston on June 19, 1865, to reestablish United States control over Texas. There he read General Order Number 3, freeing the slaves in Texas. Yet this battle fought on the muddy banks of the Sabine River has been forgotten. Obscured by time, distance and the small numbers involved, it has become one more ghostly memory on the Texas coast.

By 1863, the tide had turned against the South—except in Texas. Its Confederate commander, John Magruder, chased the Yankees out of Galveston and the Rio Grande Valley. Keeping Texas would be difficult. The Union dominated Gulf waters, allowing it to strike anywhere along Texas's four-hundred-mile coast. Texas had few railroads. Supplies followed rivers. An invasion of Texas had to come through Shreveport, Louisiana, or six ports on the Gulf Coast. Magruder had to cover the five-hundred-mile Texas coast with just 2,500 men.

One exposed spot was Sabine Pass, the outlet for the Sabine and Neches Rivers. It guarded the eastern approaches to Texas. The Union raided Sabine Pass in September 1862. Navy gunboats smashed the fort there. In spring 1863, Magruder sent Major Julius Kellersberg to Sabine City with

A statue of Dick Dowling at the Sabine Pass Battlefield Park. He died of yellow fever two years after the Civil War ended but achieved a remarkable, if all but forgotten, victory at Sabine Pass. *Author photo.*

five hundred slaves and orders to build a new fort. Kellersberg picked a spot upstream of the ruined fort, overlooking the trickiest part of the pass, a sharp bend where two narrow channels merged.

Kellersberg dug a three-sided earth embankment, reinforced with iron rails and crossties. The fort was named Fort Griffin for the local district commander. Six cannon were found. Two twenty-four-pound iron long guns and two thirty-two-pound howitzers were taken from forts upstream of Sabine Pass. Two thirty-two-pound long guns were literally unearthed. Smashed and buried when the old fort was abandoned, they were dug up and refitted.

Magruder assigned the Davis Guards, a company of the First Texas Heavy Artillery Regiment, to Fort Griffin. Forty-two strong, this Houston militia unit, raised in 1860, was composed of Irish immigrants. Their officers were Irish American merchants and tradesmen. Irish longshoremen and day laborers filled its ranks.

The Davis Guards had a reputation for being mutinous and fractious. Much of their negative reputation seems to rest on anti-Irish prejudice, common in the 1860s. The unit had been ordered disbanded and then the order countermanded. Magruder's experience with the Davis Guards was positive. They led the charge sealing Magruder's victory at Galveston.

Whether the reassignment represented a reward or an attempt to remove the brawling Irishmen from Galveston, the choice was fortunate. The men welcomed an opportunity to actually fire cannon, conducting live-fire target practice weekly. Kellersberg planted range stakes at three-hundred-yard intervals across both channels covered by the battery. By September, they could use their guns with deadly efficiency.

Magruder assigned two bay steamers, "cottonclads" *Uncle Ben* and *Josiah Bell*, armed with twelve-pound guns to guard Sabine Pass. Two unarmed transports rounded out the Confederate forces at Sabine Pass.

President Lincoln pressed Nathaniel P. Banks, commanding the Department of the Gulf, to move Union forces into Texas. Banks decided to move against Sabine Pass. Forty thousand bales of Rebel cotton lay within reach of the Sabine River. It could be seized as contraband and sold at a prize court. As department commander, Banks profited from any prize money collected.

Banks assigned four infantry brigades, six artillery batteries and several troops of the U.S. First Texas Cavalry, five thousand strong, to the task. General William Buell Franklin would command the army contingent. The navy provided seventeen transports escorted by five Union warships to carry the expedition. The escort included the deep-draft *Cayuga* and four shallow-draft gunboats capable of entering the shallow channel. All four gunboats were converted merchant vessels. The ships were lightly armored, with a mixed battery of guns.

Arizona was a 950-ton side-wheeler. It carried four thirty-two-pound smoothbores and one thirty-pound and one twelve-pound Parrott rifle. It drew ten feet. Side-wheeler *Clifton*, originally a ferryboat, displaced 892 tons. It was armed with four thirty-two-pound and two nine-inch smoothbores. It drew thirteen feet. *Granite City*, an iron-hulled side-wheeler, was 450 tons and drew nine feet, two inches. It carried four twenty-four-pound howitzers and a twelve-pound rifle. Screw-powered *Sachem* displaced 195 tons and drew seven and a half feet. It carried a twenty-pound Parrott rifle and four thirty-two-pound long guns.

Granite City was supposed to meet *Cayuga*, blockading the pass. *Granite City* would mark the mouth of Sabine Pass with a lantern visible to seaward. The rest of the fleet would leave New Orleans and rendezvous with *Granite City* at night. Eight transports would unload troops on the beach south of Sabine Pass at dawn. The four gunboats, with 170 army riflemen serving aboard as marksmen, would force the channel, silencing the fort with artillery and small arms fire. The troops landed earlier would march overland from the beaches and assault and carry the fort. From there, the Union forces would consolidate at Sabine City and then press on to Beaumont.

The plan unraveled immediately. Uninformed of the invasion, *Cayuga* left station for Galveston on September 6, 1863, for supplies. *Granite City* arrived to find the pass unguarded. *Granite City* anchored off Sabine Pass after sunset. Soon after, acting master Charles Lamson, commanding *Granite City*, spotted the Union warship *Ossipee*, steaming to join the federal blockade at Galveston. Lamson, decided the unidentified vessel was the Confederate raider *Alabama*, then thousands of miles away. Believing *Granite City* was too frail to fight *Alabama*, Lamson doused his lantern, raised anchor and slipped east. He rode out the night in the Calcusieu River, thirty-five miles east.

Two groups of transports left New Orleans on September 5. The advance group, escorted by the remaining gunboats, left first. It carried the invasion forces commanded by Brigadier General Godfrey Weitzel. They passed the Calcusieu River during the night, missing the hidden *Granite City*. Lamson either did not see these ships or ignored them. In the moonless night, the ships also missed the mouth of Sabine. The fleet steamed halfway to Galveston searching for the signal lamp before reversing course at 2:00 a.m. Dawn found them off the Louisiana coast where *Granite City* joined them.

When the advanced group finally reached the Sabine River, it was daylight. They found *Cayuga* (which returned after *Granite City*'s hasty departure) and the remaining transports anchored. Franklin decided that with the element of surprise lost, a beach landing was too dangerous. The Federal forces spent September 7 reorganizing, planning how to move the invasion forward.

The September 1863 invasion of Texas at Sabine Pass seemed unstoppable. The Union brought five thousand men and five warships mounting twenty-six cannon. The Confederacy had only forty-two artillerymen armed with six cannon to oppose them. It seemed as simple as steaming up the Sabine Pass and landing troops. *USNHHC.*

The Confederates were unsurprised and unable to resist a force the size the Federals brought. The Federal departure from New Orleans had been noticed. Garrisons along the Texas coast had been placed on full alert. At Sabine Pass, scouts were sent to the mouth of the pass, the gunners at Fort Griffin were standing by their guns and seventeen men on leave or detached service were recalled. By dawn, the scouts reported the Federal ships gathering off the coast. Captain Odlum, commanding at Sabine City, telegraphed General Magruder, reporting the scouts' findings. Feeling resistance would be futile, Magruder ordered the fort destroyed and instructed the garrison to retreat west.

Odlum passed Magruder's orders to Lieutenant Dick Dowling, commanding the fort, as permission to withdraw. A vote was taken. The gunners were spoiling to use their weapons against live targets. Dowling soon sent Odlum a response. The garrison would stay and fight.

At 6:00 a.m. on September 8, *Clifton* crossed the bar. Anchoring three-quarters of a mile from the fort, *Clifton* began bombarding the fort. Using its nine-foot Dahlgren, it fired twenty-six rounds. Two of the seventy-three-and-a-half-pound shells made direct hits on the fort. The rest were near misses. The shots went unanswered. To protect his men until the Union ships were closer, Dowling sent them the fort's bombproof shelters.

Lieutenant Frederick Crocker, captain of *Clifton* and commanding the naval warships, assumed the fort was incapacitated. At 7:30 a.m., Crocker raised anchor and steamed to the main force, reporting the fort had been silenced. By 9:00 a.m., four Federal gunboats and seven transports crossed the bar, the gunboats in the lead. The transports followed the gunboats through the channels, intending to land troops at the old fort, one thousand yards south of Fort Griffin.

While the rest of the ships anchored out of range of the fort, Franklin and Weitzel conducted a personal reconnaissance of the landing site in a ship's boat. To cover them, *Sachem* steamed slowly down the eastern Louisiana Channel. At 11:00 a.m., the Confederate cottonclad *Uncle Ben* approached the fort, steaming to one thousand yards of the boat carrying the generals. *Sachem* fired three rounds at the Confederate gunboat with its Parrott gun. *Uncle Ben* scurried back upriver.

With the reconnaissance concluded, the attack began. At 3:00 p.m., *Sachem* and *Arizona* steamed into the shallower Louisiana Channel to the east. *Clifton* and *Granite City* entered the deeper Texas Channel on the west. *Arizona*

Accurate artillery fire from the Confederate gunners quickly disabled Clifton (*left*) and Sachem (*right*), leaving both ships grounded. They were both captured after *Arizona* and *Granite City* fled. Instead of landing troops, the Union forces withdrew to New Orleans. *AC.*

had the deepest draft of the four gunboats. It lagged behind Sachem as it picked through the channel. Lamson, on *Granite City*, needed no reason to fall behind *Clifton*. He simply did.

The Union ships approached the fort individually. *Sachem* led, opening fire at two thousand yards. The Confederates held fire until *Sachem* was well inside the laid-out range stakes. Fort Griffin opened fire with *Sachem* in the narrowest stretch of the channel, within one thousand yards of the fort.

Sachem was struck by the fifth round fired. More hits followed, all clustered around the pilothouse. The ship reeled under the barrage. An unexpected crosscurrent as the ship cleared the narrows grounded the ship onto a shoal. A shot pierced *Sachem*'s steam drum. The hit flooded Sachem with live steam. The crew and its seventy-seven sharpshooters had to flee or boil. The lucky jumped overboard, into waist-deep mud.

Master Amos Johnson, commanding *Sachem*, signaled for *Arizona* to tow his ship off. *Arizona* closed to assist. It, too, came under fire and ran aground. More fortunate than Sachem, *Arizona* got a break from the fort's fire as *Clifton* closed. *Clifton* drew the fort's fire away from *Sachem* and *Arizona*. *Arizona* freed itself from the mud bank and withdrew south, abandoning *Sachem*.

Clifton closed on the fort. The fort, initially preoccupied with *Sachem* and *Arizona*, allowed *Clifton* to steam within five hundred yards of the fort unmolested. While the fort concentrated fire on the other two ships, *Clifton*'s Dahlgren carved huge chunks out of the dirt ramparts. While the hits created impressive sprays of mud, they failed to disable any of the guns. With *Arizona* and *Sachem* out of the fight, Fort Griffin turned to *Clifton*.

The first salvo missed the ironclad. Only one shot of the second volley hit Clifton. It struck astern, severing the tiller ropes. *Clifton* slewed left, grounding in a salt marsh three hundred yards from the fort.

With *Clifton* aground, Fort Griffin demonstrated excellent marksmanship. As Crocker attempted to back *Clifton* off the bank, Confederate shot raked the ship. Shots struck the boiler, spraying the decks with steam and boiling water. The forward Dahlgren was struck and damaged. The surgeon hid by the sternpost. The executive officer was killed. The second officer refused to obey Crocker's orders to fight fires, instead striking *Clifton*'s colors. Once the colors came down, the gunners abandoned ship.

Union forces could have retrieved the situation. Crocker re-hoisted his flag. *Arizona* had finally freed itself from the shoal. *Granite City* and the transport *Suffolk* were nearby. Six other transports, loaded with combat troops, were inside the bar. One Confederate gun had been dismounted. The rest were overheating. The Confederate gunners were tiring. No Confederate reinforcements were available. Committing the remaining gunboats and landing troops from the transports would have broken Texan resistance. Weitzel had troops in boats, ready to land.

Instead, *Granite City* withdrew, spreading panic. As *Granite City* passed *Suffolk*, Lamson signaled that the Confederates were bringing up horse artillery to reinforce the fort and continued south. Franklin ordered the ships withdrawn. Unsupported, *Clifton* and *Sachem* lowered their colors. Panic ensued following the order. Ships raced across the bar. Two ran aground and dumped cargo overboard to lighten the ship enough to clear the bar. By 4:30 p.m., the battle was over.

Dowling accepted *Clifton*'s surrender, wading out in waist-deep water rather than allowing the Yankees ashore where they could learn the weakness of the garrison. *Uncle Ben* took control of *Sachem*. Twenty-eight Federal soldiers and sailors were dead, seventy-five seriously wounded and over three hundred taken prisoner.

Dowling's men suffered no serious injuries. Several had burns from handling overheated guns and minor cuts from flying debris. Two guns had been struck glancing blows, but the only gun disabled was one of the howitzers, which rolled off its platform after being fired.

Sabine Pass today, a photo taken at the site of Fort Griffin. The channel has been dredged deeper than it was in 1863. Today it leads to important seaports at Beaumont, Orange and Port Arthur, Texas. *Author photograph.*

The Federal fleet—less two gunboats—returned to New Orleans, the last stragglers arriving by September 10. A Union landing at Sabine Pass was never again attempted. Instead, troops were committed to offensives along the Red River in Louisiana and Brownsville at the mouth of the Rio Grande.

To the beleaguered Texans, Sabine Pass was the Alamo refought, with Texas winning. Dick Dowling was their new Achilles. He spent the rest of the war doing the Civil War equivalent of the War Bond tour, recruiting. He died of yellow fever soon after the Civil War ended.

A Federal army at Sabine City would have knocked Texas out of the war. Franklin's five thousand men would have been quickly reinforced to fifteen thousand. Magruder lacked the forces to stop a Union advance over the coastal plain. Instead, Texas remained the only Confederate state whose heartland remained inviolate until after Appomattox.

Franklin and Banks gained ridicule for inept leadership. Franklin's reputation was hurt most, especially after he cited the strength of the Confederate resistance as a reason for his withdrawal. Most observers could not believe forty-two militia gunners bluffed five thousand soldiers.

They had. Only in Texas.

9

THE GHOST PORT
OF INDIANOLA

Indianola was once the second-biggest deep-water seaport in Texas. It rivaled mighty Galveston. Today, it is abandoned, a ghost town and a ghost port. Two devastating hurricanes, the first in 1875 and the second in 1886, led residents to abandon the town. They moved themselves and the few surviving buildings inland. Today, all that remains is a historical marker near the spot where the great ghost port of Texas stood.

Indianola was an accidental city, the by-blow of German colonization in the Republic of Texas in the 1840s. Prince Karl of Solms-Braunfels, a German nobleman, led the German migration to the Texas Hill Country, heading the efforts of the Verein zum Schutze deutscher Einwanderer in Texas (Society for the Protection of German Immigrants in Texas), also called the Adelsverein. In December 1844, he selected Indian Point in Matagorda Bay as the port of entry for the German immigrants, naming it Karlshafen (Karl's Harbor) after himself.

As a port, Karlshafen had little to recommend it besides its location. It was an open roadstead on Matagorda Bay. It offered ships little shelter from Gulf storms. It was shallow. Ships had to anchor far offshore, lightering cargos to and from the ships in small boats. But its location provided the shortest overland route to German settlements like Fredericksburg and New Braunfels. More importantly, it was the shorted overland route to San Antonio.

That was important in 1844 and became increasingly more important over the next twenty years. San Antonio was then the largest and most important city in Texas. San Antonio's river was unnavigable. It could only be reached

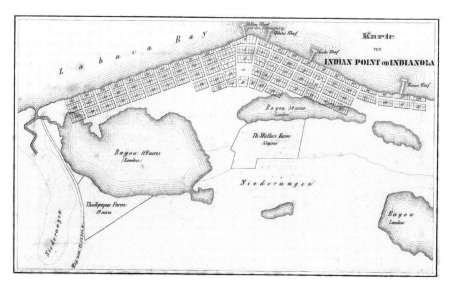

A map of Indianola shortly after it was established in 1849. This was originally published in a guide for immigrants from Germany moving to Texas's Hill Country. *AC.*

by land. In an era before railroads or automobiles, cargoes moved overland on horseback or wagon. Trips were kept as short as possible.

Some of the German immigrants purchased land on Indian point and settled there. Its first house went up in 1845. By 1846, Carlshaven was a town. When the Mexican-American War started that year, the U.S. Army established a supply depot there. It was the army's logistics center during the Mexican-American War. This depot supplied Texas frontier forts over the next three decades. It was also the start of the Chihuahua Trail, the military road that ran from San Antonio to Austin, from there to Chihuahua, Mexico and on to San Diego. Being the eastern terminus of the southern overland route to California spurred growth during the 1849 California gold rush and sustained the port thereafter.

The little port soon grew. A post office was established in 1847. Stagecoach service to the Texas interior began in 1848. Hotels went up there that same year. The name was changed to Indianola in 1849, combining *Indian* (for Indian Point) with *ola*, the Spanish word for "wave." Its first newspaper opened in 1852. Two more followed. It became the county seat for Calhoun County in 1852 with a temporary county courthouse. The city of Indianola incorporated in 1853. A permanent courthouse of shell concrete was erected in 1857, commensurate with the dignity of Indianola's role as head of county government.

By the end of the 1850s, Indianola was booming. Long wooden piers were built stretching out into Matagorda Bay, allowing deep-draft ships (by 1850s standards) to tie up and unload and receive cargos directly over the side of the ship. The Morgan Line, the Gulf Coast's biggest shipping company, built its own pier at Indianola and began scheduling runs from New York City to Texas through Indianola.

Goods heading to San Antonio unloaded at Indianola, as did the army cargoes bound for the United States' Southwest frontier. (In 1856, Indianola received a load of camels intended as the core of a U.S. Army Camel Corps. The camels were intended to carry loads across the Southwest's Chiuahuan and Sonoran Deserts.) By 1860, Indianola was beginning to rival Galveston.

Indianola had rivals in Matagorda Bay, most notably, Lavaca (today's Port Lavaca) farther up Matagorda Bay in an inlet known as Lavaca Bay. But Indianola was first and outshined Lavaca. When Lavaca started building a railroad to Victoria, Texas, in 1858, Indianola began planning its own railroad to San Antonio. By 1860, the Indianola Railroad secured financing (from Germany, still interested in investing in Texas).

The Civil War put a temporary stop to Indianola's growth. Union gunboats bombarded Indianola on October 26, 1862, and then briefly occupied and looted the port. The Union again occupied Indianola in November 1863, stationing a regiment there and remaining well into 1864. Lavaca managed to wrest the county seat from Indianola in 1864 by claiming Indianola city officials were collaborating with the Yankees.

The hard times ended in 1865, when the war and the blockade ended. The courthouse and county government returned to Indianola—so did commerce. Prior to the Civil War, Indianola had been a major port for hides and tallow. After the Civil War, it went nineteenth-century high-tech, exporting frozen meat. In 1869, a load of refrigerated beef departed Indianola for New Orleans aboard *Agnes*, a Morgan Line ship equipped with a naphtha-based refrigeration system designed by Henry Howard of San Antonio. It was the first shipment of beef from Texas—or anywhere in the world—to be artificially refrigerated from pier to pier.

Charles Morgan, who ran the Morgan Line, had big plans for Indianola in those post–Civil War years. A New York–based shipping magnate, he ran the biggest steamship company in the Gulf of Mexico during the middle of the nineteenth century. He had extensive holdings in Indianola before the Civil War. After it, he expanded them, buying up the Indianola Railroad and completing a railroad connection to San Antonio in 1871.

He planned to increase Indianola operations even more during 1873. That year, the Galveston Wharf Company, which previously allowed the Morgan Line free use of its Galveston facilities, began charging Morgan Line wharf fees. Morgan decided to bypass Galveston to the extent possible. He financed a deep-water channel to Houston, creating a seaport there. He also immediately began routing cargoes through Indianola using his railroad connection to reroute cargoes that would otherwise have gone to Galveston.

By 1875, Indianola was booming again, even more than it had in the 1850s. The population had swelled to nearly five thousand. It was threatening Galveston's supremacy as Texas's reigning seaport. In August 1875, its future seemed boundless. The next month, the hurricane hit.

The 1875 Indianola hurricane was born off the Cape Verde Islands, cradle of many deadly storms that have devastated Texas. A precursor tropical wave was first noticed on September 1 near there. By September 8, a hurricane, it was east of the Lesser Antilles. By September 12, it had passed over Haiti's southern peninsula. It marched the length of Cuba before entering the Gulf of Mexico near Havana.

It weakened to a tropical storm over Cuba but quickly gained strength over the Gulf of Mexico. Streaking almost due west, by September 15, it had grown into a major storm, one the Saffir-Simpson Scale, developed in 1971,

Indianola was the eastern end of the Sonoma Trail to the American Southwest and California. The most unusual cargo unloaded at Indianola was a load of camels imported from the Ottoman Empire to form a camel corps for the U.S. Army to move cargoes across the southwest deserts. *AC.*

classifies as a Category 3. With sustained winds estimated at 115 miles per hour, it made landfall on the Texas coast the next morning near Indianola.

The town was crowded with visitors present to empanel juries for two spectacular murder trials at the Calhoun County Courthouse. Indianola had been through several hurricanes during its short life, so no one in the courthouse worried unduly. The trials continued. Many who escaped jury duty remained to watch the trials.

This hurricane was not like the earlier storms hitting Indianola. It was a great deal more powerful. It brought a massive storm surge that created massive damage on the Texas coast. The two lighthouses marking Pass Cavallo, the entrance to Matagorda Bay and Indianola, were washed away, their keepers killed. Matagorda Island was scoured flat and those on it killed. Velasco, at the mouth of the Brazos River, the historic port of colonial Texas, was washed away.

Indianola was equally badly hammered. The storm surge covered its business district with up to six feet of water. Powerful winds, combined with the scouring action of water, undermined foundations and toppled buildings. Ships anchored in the harbor were swept inland, demolishing buildings in their path. Heavy timbers, shaken free of piers and collapsed buildings by the storm, battered other buildings.

The courthouse, with its masonry construction and a six-foot-deep foundation, proved one of the few safe refuges in the city. People crowded into it, sheltering in its second floor as the first story flooded. Wind and water blew in its windows. The two accused murderers saved several men and women during the storm by swimming to the aid of drowning people near the courthouse and dragging them back in through the open windows into the courthouse.

At 9:00 p.m. on September 16, the eye passed over Indianola. After a few minutes of calm, the winds reversed direction. The waters pushed inland and rushed back to sea, battering buildings a second time and destroying some that survived the waves' first onslaught.

Daybreak brought calm. The sun revealed a devastated Indianola. Three-quarters of its buildings had been destroyed. Most of the remaining structures were damaged. Only eight were undamaged enough to be considered habitable. The piers and harbor facilities were gone. Between 150 and 300 people in Indianola when the hurricane made landfall were dead by the morning of September 17. The storm killed a total of 800 people on the Texas coast, most as a result of the storm surge.

After the storm, there was talk of relocating the town farther up Matagorda Bay, on higher ground at a more sheltered location. Many survivors left Indianola immediately after the storm, never to return. They had had enough. The rest, one-half to two-thirds of Indianola's pre-storm population, decided to rebuild the city where it was. The courthouse was repaired. (The trials being held when the storm hit never resumed. The accused used the chaos following the storm to escape custody.)

It took time, but over the next ten years, Indianola rebuilt. It was a smaller Indianola, but by 1885, it was regaining the prosperity it had lost when the 1875 storm hit. Maybe the future promised in the summer of 1875 would really arrive.

Then it happened again. The following year, a second hurricane hit Indianola. This storm formed on August 12, 1886, just east of Trinidad and Tobago, off the northern coast of South America. It remained a tropical storm for the next two days. It hit Hispaniola as a Category 1 hurricane. Over the next four days, it passed over Hispaniola and Cuba, dipping back to a tropical storm and then growing back to a hurricane.

As it crossed the Gulf of Mexico, it grew explosively. The summer had been hot and dry, heating Gulf water well above normal. (Texas was experiencing a drought.) Crossing the Gulf, the hurricane sucked energy from the warm water. By August 20, two days after entering the Gulf of Mexico, it made landfall on the Texas coast as a Category 4 storm with sustained winds of 150 miles per hour. It was then the most powerful recorded storm to hit the U.S. coast. It made landfall near Indianola. In addition to 150-mile-per-hour winds, it arrived with a fifteen-foot storm surge.

Indianola was once again inundated. Worse, as the waters receded, fire swept the town. A lit lamp in the signal station was tipped over when the building collapsed, and a fire started. Fire soon spread to surrounding buildings. Before it burned out, Indianola's central business district was in ashes. All but two of Indianola's buildings were destroyed, and the surviving buildings were uninhabitable. The storm also washed away the two miles of railroad track closest to Indianola, making communication with the town difficult and getting supplies there almost impossible.

There was only one piece of good news. The death toll was lower, only forty-six in Indianola. The storm had approached during daytime and gave a day's warning of its approach. Many inhabitants cleared out before it arrived, and the rest found shelter. (The courthouse building withstood the second hurricane as it had the first.)

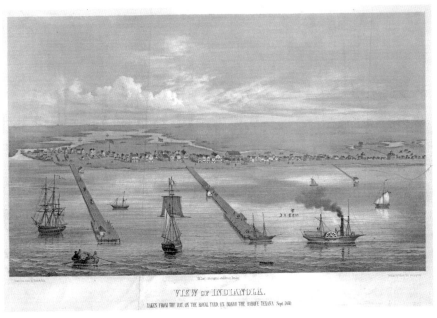

Indianola in 1860. It was already Texas's second-biggest seaport by that day. While the Civil War would interrupt its prosperity, it soon regained it during the ten years between the end of the Civil War and the 1875 Indianola hurricane. *LOC.*

But it was enough for the 1,500 residents of Indianola in 1886. They left. They moved inland, away from the coast or to more sheltered coastal communities. Indianola was never rebuilt. Lavaca achieved its goal of becoming the first city of Calhoun County when the county seat relocated there before the end of 1886. The houses still standing in Indianola were moved elsewhere, some as far away as Victoria, Texas, in adjacent Victoria County. Indianola's post office closed in October 1887, and the town was proclaimed officially "dead."

Time washed away most of the remnants of the town over the next century. The foundations of the 1857 courthouse remain, but the sands have reclaimed the rest of the buildings. You cannot even walk to the town's site. Texas's shifting coastline has moved inland from where it was at Indianola's founding. The city's port and downtown area is drowned by Matagorda Bay, one hundred yards offshore. The foundations of the courthouse can occasionally be seen at low tide. There is a granite marker commemorating the courthouse on shore and a Texas state historical plaque. The only other reminders of Texas's once second-mightiest port are memories and the ghosts of the hurricanes' dead.

10

THE FORGOTTEN
GALVESTON HURRICANE

Although hurricanes turned Indianola into a ghost town, Indianola was not the only Texas port infamous for hurricanes. Galveston, Indianola's rival for the title of chief port of Texas, suffered its own catastrophic hurricane in 1900. It was fourteen years after the 1886 hurricane, which had led to Indianola's abandonment. The 1900 storm flattened Galveston. Indianola suffered three hundred dead due to the hurricane that hit it in 1875, a number thought phenomenal. The 1900 Galveston hurricane left at least five thousand and possibly up to eight thousand dead in its wake, just in Galveston.

The storm became a cultural touchstone. It remains both the deadliest hurricane in the United States and the most famous hurricane. It is the storm by which hurricanes are compared. The Galveston hurricane overshadowed those that hit Indianola, so much so that Indianola is largely forgotten. Oddly, the next hurricane to hit Galveston is also forgotten, even though it was more powerful than the 1900 storm.

Galveston in 1900 was several orders of magnitude more important than Indianola in 1875. Indianola's population topped at 5,000 before the 1875 storm. Galveston's population, as measured by the 1900 census completed three months before the 1900 hurricane, was 37,789. It was the fourth-largest city in Texas, behind San Antonio, Houston and Dallas. It was Texas's largest seaport. In the United States, it was second in traffic only to the port of New York City. It was one of the most prosperous cities in Texas, called the "Queen City." It was also a prime vacation spot, the Oleander City, a favorite of tourists.

Galveston's 1900 hurricane leveled the town and left over five thousand dead in Galveston alone. Many Galveston residents feared Galveston would share the same fate as Indianola. *LOC.*

Then the 1900 hurricane struck. The event dethroned Galveston. Its population plunged afterward. It not only lost five thousand dead, but thousands of others left never to return. Its railroad connections were cut, electric and telephone service knocked out and water and sewer system destroyed. However, just like Indianola in 1875, Galveston was determined to rebuild.

The 1886 Indianola hurricane made Galveston aware of its vulnerability to hurricanes. If anything, it was more vulnerable than Indianola. The maximum elevation of Galveston Island in the nineteenth century was only nine feet above sea level. Unlike Indianola, sheltered by Matagorda Island, Galveston was on a barrier island, exposed to the full fury of Gulf storms.

There had been talk of building a seawall to protect Galveston following the 1886 hurricane, but it remained just talk. Building a seawall was expensive. Galveston residents comforted themselves with the belief that Galveston's location made a hit by a big hurricane unlikely. Throughout the nineteenth century, they hit the coast east and west of Galveston. The longer this went on, the more Galvestonians became convinced it would continue.

The 1900 hurricane stripped residents of those illusions. Galvestonians were also aware that Indianola was hit by a second more powerful hurricane eleven years after the first one hit it, just after Indianola finished rebuilding. Galvestonians were aware that could happen to Galveston as well. They decided to build a seawall, but they decided to do more than just that. They decided to raise the city as well.

The 1886 Indianola hurricane was the most powerful storm recorded to hit Texas during the century. Galveston decided to protect the city against a storm even more powerful. Leaders arranged construction of a seventeen-foot-tall seawall, two feet taller than the fifteen-foot storm surge that washed over Indianola. They also decided to raise the city to match that height.

Using a partnership between city, county, state and federal governments, a seventeen-foot-tall, fifteen-foot-wide seawall stretching from the eastern end of Galveston Island to Fort Crockett, four and a half miles to the west, was built. They raised the entire city using fill dredged from the harbor area. (Deepening the harbor through dredging was a win-win. It allowed the port to receive larger ships.)

Work began in 1902 and was largely finished by 1910. The city had been raised as much as 15.5 feet immediately behind the seawall, sloping down one foot for every 1,500-foot distance from the seawall. Five hundred city blocks had been raised, with 16.3 million cubic feet of sand used to do so. It was the largest civil engineering project in the history of the United States at that time and would remain the largest until the construction of the Hoover Dam in the 1930s.

By 1910, Galveston had largely recovered from the 1900 hurricane. The population as measured by the 1910 census was 36,989, only 800 fewer than before that hurricane. The rail connections had been reestablished and a new electric interurban railroad connected Galveston with Houston. Its port was busier than ever, the world's leading cotton port and the third-largest exporter of wheat.

It was beginning to face competition from Houston, fifty miles inland. Much of the cotton shipped from Galveston came from Houston in barges to be loaded onto seagoing ships in Galveston's harbor. The 1900 hurricane spurred construction of the Houston Ship Channel. That offered another motivation to deepen Galveston's harbor. It would keep Galveston on top once the Houston Ship Channel was open for business in 1914.

Galveston responded by building a seventeen-foot-tall seawall (shown under construction here) and raising the city to the level of the seawall. *LOC.*

The Port of Houston officially opened on September 7, 1914. It was not yet a serious competitor to Galveston in 1915. Shippers remained reluctant to use Houston. The first seagoing vessel would not tie up at Houston until August of 1915. Meanwhile, business at Galveston's port was booming. World War I started in August 1914, increasing demand for Galveston's chief exports: cotton, grain and sugar. Yet Galveston's seawall and hurricane defenses remained untested until 1915.

The storm formed near the Cape Verde Islands on August 5, 1915. Following a path similar to that of the 1900 Galveston hurricane, it crossed the Atlantic, emerging as a hurricane. It passed over the Lesser Antilles on August 10. Only then did U.S. weather authorities realize a storm of that magnitude was bearing down on North America.

The storm spent the next four days marching across the Caribbean, following a path eerily reminiscent of that of the 1900 storm. On August 14, it crossed the western tip of Cuba as a Category 4 hurricane, with sustained winds of 145 miles per hour. It was as large as the 1900 storm had been at that point. From there, it moved steadily across the Gulf of Mexico, maintaining its strength.

It made landfall in the early-morning hours of August 17, 1915, near San Luis Pass on the western tip of Galveston Island, twenty-six miles from the city of Galveston. By contrast, the 1900 storm landed near the center of Galveston Island. But while the landfall of the slightly stronger 1915 storm brought slightly lower winds, it also brought a higher tidal surge. In 1900, the tidal surge was estimated at 15.0 feet. In 1915, it was 16.2 feet.

The storm was a killer before it reached Galveston, having killed nearly 150 people by the time it made landfall on the Texas Coast. Everyone remembered what the 1900 storm had done to Galveston, and this was almost a perfect replica of that storm.

Galveston had plenty of warning. Hurricane reporting had improved since 1900, so the city knew a major storm was in the Gulf, with the potential to hit Galveston. Hurricane swells began reaching the island on August 15. The railroads, especially the electric interurban, began running specials to allow Galvestonians to evacuate. The last run occurred on the evening of August 17. The last Southern Pacific sleeper train headed toward Galveston was forced to stop at Seabrook, twenty-five miles from Galveston. The ultimate interurban train ended up stranded outbound at Virginia Point just after leaving Galveston Island when winds blew down the electric lines powering it.

Soon, Galveston was isolated from the world. Telegraph and telephone lines to Galveston stopped working after 9:00 p.m. on August 17. More ominously, so did wireless communications. Galveston's Marconi station, a new technology since 1900, ceased messaging as the storm reached landfall. Galveston was cut off from the world. Communications would not be restored until August 19, two days later. The world outside Galveston could only wait and wonder whether the seawall would work or whether this storm would finish Galveston, much as Indianola's second hurricane had turned that city into a ghost town.

The hurricane crawled across Galveston Island during the nighttime hours of August 17 and 18. The storm pushed up an enormous surge. Galveston was on the windward side of the storm, with the winds pushing the water onto the seawall. Crests as high as 21.0 feet were kicked up. A storm surge of 15.2 feet was recorded at Virginia Point on West Bay opposite Galveston Island. No estimate of the surge was recorded in Galveston because the gauges were destroyed by the storm.

Galveston's business district, the Strand, on the lower but sheltered north side of Galveston Island, began flooding at 6:00 p.m. By the early-morning hours of August 18, the waters had reached their height, submerging the

On August 15, 1915, Galveston was hit by a hurricane as powerful, if not a little more powerful, than the one that hit in 1900. While the waves crashed over the seawall, as shown in this picture, they failed to overtop the protective wall. *UHDL.*

streets in the business district under more than six feet of water. Afterward, by measuring high-water marks, the Army Corps of Engineers estimated the storm surge at Galveston was nearly twelve feet above mean sea level, a greater inundation than seen in 1900.

Winds peaked at about 95 miles per hour, with gusts up to 115 miles per hour. This was enough to blow down rickety, lightly built or badly built structures. Light wood-frame homes along Seawall Boulevard were blown down. Well-built structures, especially the brick and concrete construction of the business district, easily survived. The Galvez Hotel just behind the seawall suffered a few broken buildings but was otherwise undamaged. Being on the highest point on the island, it experienced little flooding. Its basements were flooded. That was it.

The seawall did its job. Every structure in Galveston in front of the seawall—unprotected by it—including beach houses, fishing piers, bath houses and a substantial casino, were destroyed. Most collapsed not due to the hurricane-force winds but because the storm surge liquefied the sand on which they were built. Undermined by the moving sand, foundations shifted, bringing down the buildings. Soon even the wreckage was scoured away by the wind. The same thing happened behind parts of the seawall. Enough water splashed over the seawall to undermine a twenty-block stretch of Seawall Boulevard.

Yet the seawall did its job. Most of the buildings in Galveston sheltered behind the seawall survived. Without waves churning saturated sand, building foundations survived. Nor could the waves carry wreckage from buildings undermined by water or blown down by wind to batter other surviving structures on the island. A major factor in the widespread destruction seen during the 1900 hurricane was mitigated by the seawall.

Similarly, ships moored to wharves in Galveston Harbor, on the island's north side, largely escaped damage, as did the wharves. Several piers, including Pier 10 and 20, suffered damage. Other ships not tied up at the wharves or moored badly broke loose and were carried by wind and water. Two large steamers, *Eton Hall* and *Harlesden*, both British-flagged and presumably enjoying a break from World War I, ended up grounding on the mainland, stranded between Virginia Point and Texas City, some dozen miles from Galveston. The U.S. Army Transport *McClelland*, a thirty-year-old, 2,800-ton steamship, broke its moorings at Pier 12 and drifted across Galveston Harbor to ground on Pelican Island.

Most of the population of Galveston Island sheltered in buildings in the business district, including an estimated five thousand at Galveston's multi-story Union Station. They had to move to upper floors as the business district flooded, but they were safe. Only eleven deaths occurred in the city protected by the seawall.

The areas unsheltered by the seawall fared much worse. Of the 250 homes on Galveston Island west of the Galveston Seawall, 90 percent were destroyed by the storm. Outside the city, forty-two fatalities occurred. Fort Crockett, at the end of the seawall, suffered extensive damage due to water undermining the ground behind the seawall where it ended. Twenty-four other ships outside Galveston Harbor, including the four-mast schooner *Crockett*, capsized or wrecked during the storm.

The coastal region of Texas behind Galveston Island also suffered heavy damage. Seabrook was almost completely destroyed. Texas City suffered extensive damage. Houston took $1 million in damage. Most of the cotton crop in Harris and Brazoria Counties was destroyed. Total fatalities in Texas outside Galveston Island reached 222. It was a far cry from the 5,000 dead on Galveston fifteen years earlier.

The seawall saved Galveston from sharing the fate of Indianola. Over subsequent years, it was extended to its present length of ten miles, affording protection to twice as much of Galveston Island as it did in 1915. The 1915 Galveston hurricane did a lot of property damage in Galveston, in excess of $8 million in 1915 dollars, much in shipping destroyed and dry goods

The seawall protected those behind it. Only eleven people sheltered behind it died. It was unable to prevent major damage on the north side of the island, however. The hurricane washed away all of the bridges on the causeway linking Galveston Island to the mainland. *UHDL.*

flooded and ruined. Yet the storm was quickly forgotten. It simply did not compare to the 1900 storm.

While Galveston seemed saved, the 1915 storm ensured Galveston never regained its former prominence. Communications with Galveston were cut off for weeks. The bridges and causeways were destroyed and had to be rebuilt. While Texas fortunes in the nineteenth century were made through shipping and agricultural products, the twentieth century saw the rise of manufacturing fortunes. Businesses were willing to ship cargoes through Galveston—at least over the first thirty years after the 1915 hurricane—but they were unwilling to build major factories or refineries on the island.

Those went up on the mainland. Eventually, much of the shipping did, too, as the Port of Houston expanded. It was simpler to move goods to Houston than to Galveston. Galveston began a long, gradual decline until it transformed into a tourist and college town in the late 1980s.

THE GHOST FLEET OF THE EMERGENCY FLEET CORPORATION

The American humorist Don Marquis once observed, "When a politician does get an idea, he usually gets it all wrong." He might have been thinking about the U.S. government's World War I–era Emergency Fleet Corporation when he wrote this. It certainly qualifies as getting an idea all wrong. It left Texas waterways haunted by ghosts of abandoned ships as well as provided Galveston with one of its signature landmarks.

In some ways, it is an example of one bad idea piled on another bad idea. To compound the folly, the bad ideas were spread across multiple governments. Great Britain and the United States each contributed to this World War I tragicomedy of errors.

The United States entered World War I in 1917 due to Germany conducting unlimited submarine warfare. Through the first half of 1917, German U-boats were racking up record sinking of Allied merchant ships. They were sinking so many that the U-boats were about to starve Great Britain out of the war.

There were two ways to solve the problem. You could reduce the rate U-boats were sinking cargo ships to below the rate at which new construction replaced ships sunk. Or you could increase the production of cargo ships to the point that it did not matter how many ships the U-boats sank.

Of the two choices, the first was better. The more ships sunk the more cargoes ended up being delivered to the ocean floor rather than Europe. Cutting losses not only reduced the number of ships you had to build but also the amount of replacement cargo that had to be created.

The toll German U-boats were taking on the shipping of the western Allies during World War I threatened to starve out Britain. *USNHHC.*

It turned out there was a really simple way to reduce losses due to U-boats: convoys. Convoys had been successfully used for centuries to reduce the loss of merchant ships. But to naval officers, convoys were boring. Convoys were defensive, and proper officers were offensive-minded. Royal Navy officers gained glory (and promotion) through fighting enemy warships, not serving as beat cops patrolling a convoy. The Royal Navy claimed there were too many merchant sailings to permit convoys. They resisted instituting a convoy system until May 1917, when losses increased to the point that Great Britain had only six weeks' worth of grain stored.

The "too many ships sailing" was the first bad idea. This total included short coastal and interior waterway sailings. When only oceangoing ships were counted, the sailings dropped to manageable numbers. Moreover, World War I U-boats sank ships mainly with their deck guns because they carried few torpedoes. They could use only deck guns against merchantmen sailing individually. These U-boats were too fragile to slug it out with gunfire against a convoy, even if one with only armed merchantmen.

Simply convoying ships meant U-boats had to use torpedoes, which cut losses dramatically. And the larger the convoy, the fewer ships were sailing independently, offering fewer opportunities for U-boats to find targets. Once ships began sailing in convoy, losses to U-boats dropped to almost nothing. Had the Royal Navy instituted convoys a year earlier, the German U-boat offensive would likely have come to nothing.

The effectiveness of convoys lay in the future when the United States entered the war. Seeing the vast losses of shipping, the U.S. Congress decided to exercise the second solution: build as many new ships as possible. It created the Emergency Fleet Corporation on April 16, 1917, ten days after declaring war on the German Empire. Part of its mission was to oversee merchant ship construction in the United States.

The Emergency Fleet Corporation did some good work. It facilitated construction of modern, steel-hulled cargo ships in existing shipyards, producing standardized designs. It also saw to construction of four brand-new shipyards to mass produce merchant ships. These government-sponsored yards eventually produced a quarter of the steel-hull cargo ships and transports built in the United States during World War I. That achievement is more remarkable when you consider it had to build the shipyards first and U.S. involvement lasted only nineteen months. The ships churned out from these yards became known as Hog Islanders, after the largest yard. They dominated commercial shipping until World War II.

But the Emergency Fleet Corporation was not satisfied. It wanted enough ships to (in the slogan it coined) "build a bridge of ships" to France. It could not make more steel-hulled ships—U.S. steel mills were already running flat out. It decided to make ships from nonstrategic materials—wood and concrete.

The Emergency Fleet Corporation planned construction of roughly one thousand wooden-hulled ships during World War I. Some of the wooden ships were sailing ships but the vast majority used Emergency Fleet Corporation Design 1001, a 3,500-ton steamship with a "three island" design, the then-standard small freighter design: three superstructure "islands" on the forecastle and stern and amidships with cargo hatches in between the islands. Despite being made of wood, not steel, ships became known as "Ferris" ships. The name came from the designer, naval architect Theodore E. Ferris. Ferris ships built nationwide consumed enough pine to literally build a wooden bridge stretching from New York City to Brest, France.

Intended to be built from nonstrategic materials, these steamships were equipped with coal-fired reciprocating steam engines. This technology was being phased out in favor of oil-fired boilers and steam turbines, but the United States had plenty of capacity to build new triple-expansion engines without endangering other priorities. Additionally, nontraditional wood

The SS *Cross Keys* was one of the first wooden-hulled Ferris ships constructed during World War I. The ships appeared too late to materially contribute to the war and were worthless afterward. *AC.*

was to be used: loblolly, longleaf and yellow pine. These softwoods were in abundance on the Gulf Coast, Pacific Northwest and Maine.

Moreover, each of those areas had shipbuilding industries focused on building wooden ships. Those shipyards had slack capacity. The only wooden warships being built were small vessels such as subchasers and minesweepers. By involving existing shipyards already building wooden ships for Ferris ships, the Emergency Fleet Corporation could swell total cargo tonnage available to the Allied forces without taking away from more critical needs.

Nine Texas shipyards, one in Rockport, two each in Houston and Orange and four in Beaumont, Texas, were contracted to build Ferris ships. Additionally, two yards in Orange, Texas, familiar with building wooden sailing ships received contracts to make those. In all, Texas shipyards were supposed to build over forty wooden Ferris boats and another fourteen wooden sailing ships.

Construction of the wooden fleet was tacked on *after* expanding construction of steel ships. The thinking was that even if U-boats continued to sink ships at the rate they had been, there would be enough replacements available that total cargo capacity would actually increase. No one much cared if the wooden ships were sunk by U-boats. If a U-boat wasted a torpedo on a Ferris boat, that was one less "real" steel-hulled cargo ship sunk. Ferris ships were disposable, intended to serve an emergency need.

It seemed like such a good idea.

The war ended much sooner than anyone anticipated. Moreover, one reason it ended so much sooner was that the U-boat threat had been largely neutralized by August 1917, just when the Ferris program was gathering speed. Once fully implemented, convoys reduced shipping losses so precipitously that a surplus of steel-hulled ships was developing even before the war ended.

Then the war ended. Shipyards, including those in Texas, were only just beginning to deliver Ferris ships. With the war over, no one wanted them. They were made from wood, which leaked and rotted. They were also flammable. Since they were coal-fired, the firebox was constantly open so you could shovel in more coal. If a live coal or two bounced out of the firebox of a conventional steel ship, it landed on some steel deck plates, where it harmlessly burned out. On a wooden ship? Can you say tinderbox?

Shipping companies wanting a new cargo ship could grab some of the scads of Hog Islanders and other new construction steel vessels coming off shipways. Why get a 3,500-ton coal-fired wooden freighter fitted with reciprocating engines when there were plenty of 7,800-ton to 13,400-ton oil-fired, turbine-engine Hog Islanders available?

The Ferris ships were suddenly white elephants after hostilities ceased in November 1918. Soon after, the government canceled construction of wooden ships still on the building ways. In the Gulf District, which included Texas and Louisiana, the EFC canceled forty-nine vessels, sixteen of which were under construction. Then in May 1919, the EFC decided to dispose of all of its wooden ships, complete or incomplete. At first, the EFC asked $75,000 per vessel, exclusive of the engines. No one wanted them at that price. The white elephant fleet remained in the yards that had built them. In Texas, most of these ships were in Beaumont and Orange.

After two years, the idea finally dawned on the federal government that they were going to recover very little of the $100 million they spent building the Ferris ships. (They had spent $10 million in Texas alone.) They decided to auction off the ships. In Beaumont, the highest bidder was the Pendleton brothers. Their winning bid was $21,000, which gained them twenty-six Ferris ships in various stages of completion. Auctions elsewhere yielded similar results.

The Pendleton brothers were shipbrokers, chandlers, shipowners and insurance agents operating out of New York. They planned to remove the

After the war, most Ferris ships were towed up river estuaries and allowed to sink. This is the wreck of one Ferris ship abandoned in Neches River in the 1920s and posing a hazard to navigation in the twenty-first century. *Mark Underhill photograph.*

engines and superstructure from their purchases, converting them into barges carrying bulk cargoes, generally petroleum. Around six Gulf District Ferris ships went through that transformation, including *Unita*, built in Morgan City, Louisiana.

But these conversions proved unsuccessful. Wooden ships were too fragile to last long as barges. Some, including *Unita*, ended up wrecked. *Unita* sank after being pushed into a jetty at Corpus Christi.

The Pendleton brothers might have successfully converted a few ships into barges, but by 1924, they tired of the effort and sold their remaining twenty-two ships. By then, the ships were lining the banks of the upper Neches River north of Beaumont. The purchaser, B.F. Zellers, planned to scrap the ships for their timber. He contracted with local salvors to remove the metal from the hulks. Instead, once the metal was stripped from the ships, they were allowed to burn and sink at their moorings—or simply sink at their moorings.

There this ghostly fleet remains. Most of the hull and superstructure above water is gone, prey to ninety-plus years of storms sweeping the upper Texas coast. The remains of some can be seen when water levels are low. Others, while completely covered, pose a hazard to navigation. Boaters have had the bottoms ripped out of their boats passing over the wrecks. Unfortunately, these wrecks will continue to haunt Texas waterways around Orange and Beaumont. They have been there for nearly a century—so long the wrecks are now archaeological sites protected by the State of Texas.

There is a weird coda to this already strange tale. As mentioned earlier, the EFC experimented with concrete hulls as well as wooden hulls for ships. The EFC ordered twenty-four concrete-hull tankers during World War I, of which twelve were completed. None were built in Texas, although one ended up there. The SS *Selma* was a 6,826-gross-register ton tanker built at F.F. Ley and Company in Mobile, Alabama. Construction started before World War I ended, but the ship was not launched until June 1919. It was really a marvelous piece of engineering. The EFC leased *Selma* to a commercial operator. The brand-new vessel entered service as a tanker in the Gulf of Mexico, where it served successfully for nearly a year.

People often scoff at the notion of concrete-hull ships. After all, concrete sinks—but so do iron and steel. Like steel-hulled ships, concrete-hulled ships depend on the buoyancy of the volume inside the hull to stay afloat. You can also make complex curves more easily with concrete than metal, so for a while, concrete was used to build hulls for sailing yachts, including racing yachts.

The problem with concrete is that it is almost impossible to economically patch a hole in a concrete hull. With steel, you cut out the old plates, weld or rivet in new plates and you are done. This is not so with concrete. On May 31, 1920, the inevitable happened to *Selma*. It hit a jetty too hard docking at Tampico, Mexico, knocking a sixty-foot crack in the hull.

The operators hustled *Selma* to the nearest port with major repair facilities, Galveston, Texas. The pumps barely kept ahead of the water let in through the crack. At Galveston, they got more bad news. The dockyard had no idea how to patch the leak. It could be done, but not by them, and not cheaply.

The operators were leaking money trying to keep the ship afloat. They had to rent extra pumps and pay for the fuel to keep the pumps running to stay ahead of the incoming water. They finally chose to simply abandon the ship. After all, in 1922, there was a glut of surplus ships available. They returned *Selma* to the EFC. The EFC turned it over to the U.S. Coast Guard.

Selma weighed over thirteen thousand tons and was 420 feet long and nearly 40 feet tall from keel to deck. (It drew 26 feet fully loaded.) Did we mention it was made of concrete? The hull was only 4 to 5 inches thick,

The remains of the concrete-hull tanker *Selma* can be seen today off Galveston's Pelican Island. The ship proved impossible to patch or scrap, so it was beached to prevent it from blocking navigation channels. *William Lardas photograph.*

but if it sank in the Houston Ship Channel—or anywhere in Galveston Harbor—it would take explosives to clear the wreck. To remove this hazard to navigation, the Coast Guard had a 25-foot-deep channel hastily dredged near Galveston's Pelican Island, well away from navigation lanes. On March 22, 1922, Selma was towed into the channel and allowed to sink.

It remains there to this day, Galveston's concrete ship. It turns out concrete is about as durable as it is hard to patch. The top of the hulk remains above sea level. It was the object of several failed attempts to use it commercially, most notably as a party site and a fishing pier. The ship remains visible today. The Galveston-Bolivar ferry passes close to Selma during its passage, a mute reminder of the Emergency Fleet Corporation.

12

THE LOST LYKES LINE

When people think of Texas business giants, they think of oil barons and cattle kings, not shipping magnates. Yet one of the largest family-owned shipping lines operated out of Texas—the Lykes Brothers Steamship Line. It was not just the largest shipping company operating out of Texas. For a while, it was the largest family-owned business in the United States and the world and one of the world's largest shipping companies. If everything is bigger in Texas, that once included its shipping companies. Lykes was once larger even than Cunard, with greater gross tonnage and many more ships. (Admittedly, Cunard was more famous, more glamorous and had much larger ships.)

Today it is gone, a corporate ghost haunting the Texas Coast. It has been largely forgotten, even in Texas.

The brothers founding the Lykes Line were cattlemen. They came from Florida and came by their interest in the sea through their family. Their maternal grandfather, James McKay, was a Scots sea captain who relocated to the American South in the 1840s, operating out of Mobile, Alabama, and the Florida Gulf coast. His daughter married Dr. Howell T. Lykes, who ran cattle and raised citrus in Florida. After the Civil War, Lykes began shipping his cattle to Cuba using his father-in-law's ships. Eventually, Dr. Lykes bought out his aging father-in-law, forming his own shipping line.

The Spanish-American War decimated Cuban cattle herds. When it ended, the good doctor cleaned up shipping cattle to restore Cuba's herds. In 1900, his two oldest sons, Frederick E. Lykes and Howell T. Lykes Jr.,

The seven Lykes Brothers in the early 1920s. *POHA.*

established themselves as Cuban cattle brokers, as Lykes Brothers. They bought ranchland in Cuba and started running herds of their own on that island. Their Cuban holdings soon included a meatpacking plant. In 1900, they purchased a three-masted schooner, which they christened *Dr. Lykes* after their father. The family incorporated their Florida interests as Lykes Company.

A third brother, James McKay Lykes (named for granddad), soon joined the brothers in Cuba, and Texas enters the story. In 1903, he made a cattle-buying trip to Texas. He liked what he saw and continued making trips to Galveston to buy cattle. Pretty soon, he was sending Cuban sugar to Texas sugar mills on the return trips. In 1906, he joined Lykes Brothers as a partner and set up a shipping office in Galveston. Soon, Lykes was running a ship from Galveston to Havana every eight days. Routes to Mexico, Costa Rica, Honduras and Venezuela soon followed. Brother Lipscomb also joined the firm in 1906.

The brothers soon realized that while selling cattle turned a nice profit, shipping goods was an even better way to make money. In 1907, the Lykes Brothers consolidated with H. Mosie and Company to form Southern Shipping Lines. By 1909, the remaining three brothers, John Wall Lykes,

Thompson M. Lykes and Joseph T. Lykes, joined the firm. In 1910, the brothers reorganized once again, consolidating all the family holdings—steamship interests, cattle business and citrus orchards—into one company, Lykes Brothers Inc. Thompson became president of the family firm.

By the time World War I started, Lykes was a thriving regional shipping company servicing Caribbean and Gulf ports. World War I, surprisingly, gave the company a boost, especially after the United States entered the war. It chartered government-owned steamships, taking them on routes assigned by the United States Shipping Board. It gave Lykes valuable experience outside the Gulf of Mexico and Caribbean. It proved useful because after World War I ended, the Cuban cattle market, long Lykes's bread-and-butter, collapsed.

After World War I, the United States government sold off its war-construction cargo ships. Many were operated under lease by commercial shipping companies that did not wish to risk owning the vessels. The Lykes brothers plunged in, buying the government-owned ships they managed and those managed by the Dixie and Southern States Lines. In 1922, Lykes incorporated the Lykes Brothers Steamship Company as a Louisiana corporation. Its headquarters was in New Orleans, while Lykes Brothers Inc. kept its headquarters in Tampa.

Despite the out-of-state headsheds, Lykes shipping operations were firmly rooted in Texas. James M. Lykes, president of Lykes Steamships, moved to Texas and ran the company from there. Lykes continued operating out of Galveston, but James Lykes chose Houston for his head office—and the main focus of Lykes operations in Texas. While it seems the obvious choice today, in 1922, it was visionary.

Galveston was Texas's major seaport and had been since the Republic of Texas. The Houston Ship Channel, finished in 1914, had opened Houston as a deep-water port, but in 1922, it shipped fewer cargoes than Galveston. But Houston had much more room for growth and was vastly more accessible to rail connections than Galveston. Had Lykes continued to use Galveston as its main Texas terminal, its growth would have been constrained.

And the Lykes Line continued growing. It purchased Tampa Interocean outright in 1925. Over the next decade, it expanded service. By 1936, it had moved beyond the Gulf and Caribbean, with regular service to the British Isles, northern Europe, the Far East, the Canal Zone and the Atlantic coast of the United States. It had sixty-seven ships that could carry over 500,000 deadweight tons. A family-owned company owned one-sixth of all American flag dry cargo ships, running cargoes from the Gulf to everywhere in the world.

Lykes ships were marked by the Lykes "blue diamond" on the funnel. It was a blue diamond with a white *L* in the center on a white band on the ship's funnel. *Author photograph.*

The family stamped its personality on its ships. While ships acquired through merger or that had entered the company through United States Shipping Board charters had a wide variety of names, those built for or purchased directly by Lykes Brothers were named after family members. Starting with *Almeria Lykes* in 1922, the brothers began naming ships for female members of the family. As those ran short, they added the names of male Lykes to their ships.

The funnels of Lykes ships carried a broad white band on which the company's logo was emblazoned: a blue diamond with a large white *L*. That was how steamship companies traditionally identified their ships. But Lykes also began branding the ships of the Lykes Steamships, regardless of the ship's name, with "Lykes Line" in white large capital letters on the midships of the black-painted hull. Except during World War II, it continued the tradition as long as the family owned the Lykes Line.

By the mid-1930s, Lykes's fleet was getting old. Many of the ships acquired in the 1920s and through the early 1930s were World War I veterans. They were bargains, but they were slow and beginning to require additional maintenance. In 1936, using subsidies authorized by the new Merchant

Marine Act, the company ordered another twenty-eight new ships. It was the largest order ever placed by a steamship company.

The ships were the latest, greatest designs in U.S. shipping, using United States Maritime Commission designs. The ships were fast yet economical. Nearly five hundred feet long, they carried between 6,500 and 8,000 tons of cargo. The first, launched in 1940, was named *Frederick Lykes* after the oldest brother. It was assigned to run between Gulf ports, including Houston and the Far East. The next three of these ships, *Dr Lykes*, *Almiria Lykes* (the second Lykes ships to bear those names) and *Howell Lykes*, were also assigned to the Pacific run.

By the time the United States entered World War II, sixteen of these ships had already been delivered. World War II changed everything, fueling further growth. In 1939, war in Europe closed ports in the war zones. In early 1940, Lykes was advertising in Houston's *Port Magazine* (the trade magazine for the Port of Houston) that Lykes Orient Line (China), Lykes Continental Line (servicing Continental Europe's Atlantic and North Sea coasts), Lykes UK Line and Lykes Mediterranean Line services were suspended on account of war.

Ships no longer sailing to those ports were rerouted to new markets. The same advertisement touted a new Lykes service: Lykes Africa Line, offering regular steamship service from Houston and other Gulf ports to South and East Africa. Similarly, Lykes increased traffic to other Far East ports in British and Dutch possessions. U.S. demand for raw tin and rubber kept Lykes ships busy hauling these commodities through November 1941.

When the United States finally entered World War II, Lykes Line's fortunes again changed, yet again for the better. The brothers ran an efficient, effective

By the 1950s, the Lykes Line was one of the world's largest shipping lines. Here, five Lykes Line cargo ships are tied up at the Port of Houston in 1949. *UHDL.*

company and wholeheartedly supported the war effort. The government gave Lykes construction priority and assigned Lykes to manage many new war-construction merchant vessels. Lykes lost several ships during the war, most to U-boats. (One was expended as a breakwater for the artificial harbor built at Normandy after the 1944 D-Day landings.) But the vast majority of these were its older ships, which were replaced by new construction. Lykes owned or operated 125 cargo ships and handled sixty million tons of cargo during World War II.

After World War II, Lykes sold off its older ships, replacing them with twenty-one new cargo ships purchased as government surplus. By the 1950s, it owned fifty cargo ships. Eleven belonged to the U.S. Naval Reserve Fleet. These ships were approved for use as naval auxiliaries during national emergencies, cementing the relations Lykes developed with the navy during World War II and providing the corporation a useful subsidy.

Lykes was well placed to capitalize on the postwar boom. The Port of Houston's location on the central Gulf made it a convenient arrival and departure point for anything bound to or from the United States between the Appalachian and Rocky Mountains. The central United States was the nation's industrial and agricultural heartland. The port grew explosively during the 1950s, and Lykes was there.

Lykes revived and expanded its prewar services. By 1950, Lykes had seven subsidiaries operating out of Houston: Lykes West Indies and South American Line, Lykes Africa Line, Lykes UK Line, Lykes Continental Line and Lykes Orient Line. It also controlled Delta Line and Mississippi Shipping Company and served as Houston agents for three other major steamship lines. Lykes could ship to 156 ports. If you wanted to ship anywhere in the world by sea from Houston in the 1950s, you could reach it through Lykes.

By the late 1950s, Lykes's fleet, which dated to World War II, was getting old. Just as it had twenty years earlier, Lykes embarked on an ambitious expansion and replacement project. In 1958, Lykes laid plans to replace its entire fleet with fifty-three new ships. The building program would last fourteen years and consume a $500 million (in 1960 dollars). It was a serious investment in the future, even though the Federal Maritime Board subsidized the venture. (The ships would be part of the U.S. Naval Reserve Fleet.) The Lykes took Lykes Steamship Inc. public in 1958, in part to finance the new program.

The first five keels were laid in 1959, to be delivered in 1960. All were to be built in the United States. (They had to be, thanks to the 1920 Jones Act, which mandated U.S. flag ships be made in the States.) They were based on the latest U.S. Maritime Administration (MARAD) designs. They were bigger, faster and more reliable than the previous generation of Lykes ships, built two decades earlier. They were also obsolescent when their keels entered the water.

The ships were break-bulk vessels, as all general dry-cargo steamships had been for over a century. Cargoes were stored on pallets in crates or bales and loaded by hand into the ship. It took weeks to load and unload a ship this way, and cargo ships often spent more time in port than at sea. But it was the way things always had been done.

In 1956, Macomb MacLean upended "the way things always had been done." He sent a shipload of cargo packed in shipping containers, boxes that could be carried on ships or the back of flatbed trucks or rail cars. The port of destination was Houston.

The container revolutionized shipping. It cut cargo-handling costs by an incredible 97 percent. It reduced the time it took to unload or load a ship from weeks to hours. It expedited shipment even after it left the ship, as the cargo could be taken in truckload lots to its destination. It took twenty years for the container to take over, but even as *James Lykes*, the first of the new generations of Lykes ships, entered service, the container's advantages were becoming obvious.

Containerization required specially designed ships, with hatches large enough to accommodate rows of containers. Conventional break-bulk cargo ships of the 1950s and 1960s could not economically carry containers. Their hatches were too small. They could carry containers as deck cargo, but only in small numbers—too small to break even. Lykes had been wrong-footed by the change.

Lykes did quickly change to container ships. But it had to play catch-up to SeaLand, the first container line, founded by Malcomb MacLean after that first cargo of containers arrived in Houston. Instead of being the dominant U.S. shipping company, Lykes was becoming number two. Lykes tried to leapfrog the container by developing LASH (Lighter Aboard SHip) vessels, ships designed to carry river barges. But in this case, bigger was not better. Containers were more practical, and Lykes end up selling off the LASH ships it had.

But the brothers who founded the company were departing. By 1960, only one was still alive. The family—now managed by a new generation—maintained control of Lykes, even after it went public. The shipping industry was also changing. The Lykes family adapted, but it became increasingly difficult for American flag ships to compete in the global economy. In 1979, the Lykes sold

Lykes invested heavily in building a series of fast break-bulk cargo liners in the late 1950s and early 1960s, like this one, the *James Lykes*. They were obsolescent when launched due to the appearance of container ships. *Author photograph.*

their remaining interest in shipping and retreated back to their Florida citrus and cattle interests.

Yet they could not resist the lure of the sea. The Lykes family repurchased the company in 1983. They could not recapture the old magic, however, and the company began a downhill slide to bankruptcy. Canadian Pacific Ships Limited purchased the company in 1997. The Lykes flag finally disappeared in 2005, when Canadian Pacific reflagged all of its ships under its own brand.

13

THE GHOSTS OF
SEAWOLF PARK

Galveston's Seawolf Park is one of the city's important maritime tourist draws. Tens of thousands come every year to visit it and tour its two principal attractions: the Edsall-class destroyer escort *Stewart* and the Gato-class submarine *Cavalla*. Both are important relics of World War II. *Stewart* is one of two surviving World War II destroyer escorts in the United States.

Cavalla is not as unique. There are ten U.S. Navy submarines from World War II, including six Gato-class submarines, preserved as museums. But *Cavalla* has one unique distinction: it sank the Japanese aircraft carrier *Shokaku* during 1944's Battle of the Philippine Sea. *Shokaku* was one of six Japanese carriers participating in the December 7, 1941, and the only one sunk by a submarine.

There are some other exhibits at the park. At one time, it had a F-4J Sea Fury, an M-41 Walker Bulldog light tank and an LVTP-5 armored landing craft, but those are long gone. The sail from the nuclear attack submarine USS *Tautog* (SSN-639) and the conning tower from the Balao-class USS *Carp* are on display. So is a navy whaler, the type of boat carried aboard the *Stewart* and its sister destroyer escorts during World War II. A very similar whaler carried a boarding party from the destroyer escort *Pillsbury* (another Edsall-class ship) to capture the *U-505* in World War II. You can also view the wreck of the SS *Selma*, Galveston's concrete ship from the fishing pier.

Still, the main reason most come to Seawolf Park, if not to fish, is to see the *Stewart* and *Cavalla*. *Cavalla*, the submarine, came first. It was joined in 1976 by the destroyer escort *Stewart*. The two vessels are worth seeing. The

Seawolf Park is best known for its main displays: the destroyer escort *Stewart* and the submarine *Cavalla*. *William Lardas photograph.*

casual visitor might wonder, however, why the place is called Seawolf Park. There is no vessel named *Seawolf* in or near the park. Except in memory.

Seawolf Park started out as Seawolf Memorial Park. It was built to commemorate USS *Seawolf* (SS-197), lost during World War II. (That was a major reason *Cavalla* came to the park first. It memorialized the other submarine.) But *Seawolf* was largely overlooked during the park's opening years. There was a memorial built to *Seawolf*, but in the late 1970s and early 1980s, it was located by the Battleship Texas at the San Jacinto Battlefield Park in La Port, Texas. (It was moved to Seawolf Park in the 1990s.)

Seawolf Park made up for that neglect over the last twenty-five years. The portion of the park containing *Stewart* and *Cavalla* was rededicated as the Galveston Naval Museum and as the American Undersea Warfare Center. Moreover, the purpose of the Galveston Naval Museum was formally expanded from memorializing *Seawolf* to remembering the other fifty-one U.S. submarines lost during World War II and the U.S. submarines lost due to accident in the years since 1945.

The most visible evidence of this is a plaza located between *Stewart* and *Cavalla*, installed during the rehabilitation of the Seawolf Park to repair damage left by Hurricane Ike in 2006. Surrounded by low concrete benches, the plaza contains a stone compass rose, mimicking the compass card traditionally used by every ship. In the outer ring, equally spaced, are metal plaques for each of the submarines lost during World War II. Two other plaques, outside the ring, commemorate the lost nuclear submarines *Thresher* and *Scorpion*.

Each plaque contains the name of the submarine, its US Navy number, the date it was lost, the number of crew that died when it was sunk and the location of its lost. At the bottom of each plaque is an image of the World War II version of submariner's dolphins, the badge awarded to a sailor when he qualifies for the submarine service.

Most plaques contain the simple statement "All Hands Lost." It was the price of submarine warfare. Every U.S. submarine lost while submerged was lost with all hands. Even if it was surfaced when it was sunk, generally, survivors were limited to those who were on deck when the submarine went down for the last time. Even in those cases, there was no guarantee those left stranded on the ocean's surface would later be rescued. Some were left to die on the ocean. And only once during all of World War II did U.S. submariners escape from a submarine sitting on the ocean bottom. Even then, less than a dozen men escaped from that submarine—USS *Tang*.

In total, of the 16,000-plus U.S. Navy sailors who served aboard submarines in World War II, nearly 3,500 died in combat, over 1 man in 5. It was the highest percentage of men lost on every major category of warship in the United States Navy in World War II and a greater percentage of loss in any branch of the US Navy. The ghosts of all of these men are remembered at Seawolf Park.

These men were all volunteers. That was the only way to serve on a submarine. You had to volunteer for duty and successfully complete training just to qualify for duty aboard a submarine. To receive submariner's dolphins, a prospect has to complete qualifications, with the prospect's progress recorded on a qualification booklet—the "qual card." Qualifying made you part of a navy elite. The navy remembers those lost on submarine duty as being on eternal patrol.

Seawolf is remembered individually. Its World War II career is recorded on a plaque mounted vertically at the right end of the Memorial Walkway in the Undersea Warfare Center. On the left is a plaque listing all of the Submarines "Still on Patrol" due to being lost in World War II. In between these are two other plaques—one listing the names of the eighty-three submariners and the other the seventeen U.S. Army personnel aboard *Seawolf* when it was lost.

Seawolf Park's memorial circle for U.S. Navy submarines lost at sea. The park also has plaques honoring *Seawolf* and the men lost aboard *Seawolf* on its fifteenth war patrol. *Author photograph.*

Why *Seawolf?* USS *Seawolf* (SS- 197) might have been the U.S. Navy's most outstanding submarine. *Seawolf* racked up a remarkable record in the thirty-four months it fought for the United States in the Pacific during World War II. *Seawolf* certainly qualifies as the navy's fightingest submarine. It ranked fourteenth in total tonnage sunk and tenth in ships sunk. It conducted fifteen combat patrols, tied with the submarines *Narwhal*, *Thresher* and *Gar* and exceeded only by *Stingray*'s sixteen. *Seawolf* began its first war patrol on December 8, 1941, and finished its last on October 3, 1944. It might have spent more days on combat patrol than any other United States Navy submarine.

Its loss was also the most tragic of all U.S. submarine losses in World War II. It was the only submarine confirmed lost due to friendly fire. (A second submarine, USS *Dorado* [SS-248] was believed to have been sunk in the Caribbean by a U.S. Navy aircraft. Its actual cause of loss is ambiguous, and it might actually have been sunk by a minefield laid by one of two German U-boats in the area through which *Dorado* passed.) A U.S. Navy warship sank *Seawolf* on the submarine's fifteenth and final war patrol.

Seawolf was a Sargo-class submarine, one of the last classes of submarines built prior to U.S. entry into World War II. These boats (submarines are always called boats—even nuclear ballistic missile submarines bigger than some battleships that saw service in World War II) displaced 1,450 tons surfaced and 2,350 tons submerged. They were 310½ feet long and had a beam of 26 feet and 10 inches.

They were powered by four electric motors that drove two propellers. These boats could move at up to 21 knots on the surface and 8¾ knots submerged. Running at top speed submerged would run its batteries flat in less than an hour, but it could travel submerged at 2 knots for forty-eight hours. Seawolf charged the batteries (or ran the electric motors) using one to four General Motors V-16 diesel engines that were hooked up to electric generators.

Seawolf was armed with eight torpedo tubes, four forward and four aft. It carried twenty-four torpedoes with eight already in the tubes and two reloads for each tube. It carried a three-inch, fifty-caliber deck gun aft of the coning tower and mounted four machine guns on the conning tower. At the start of World War II, it carried a crew of fifty-nine—five officers and fifty-four men. During the war, that would grow by over twenty as new equipment, such as radar, was added to Seawolf. It left its submariners almost as packed as sardines in a tin.

Seawolf was not as capable as the war-built Gato and Balao classes of U.S. submarines. It had two fewer torpedo tubes and could not dive as deep. But it had the same range and endurance. Even if the Sargo-class and the successor Tambor-class were less capable than war-built boats, they were what was available when Japan attacked Pearl Harbor, the U.S. possessions in the Philippines and elsewhere in the Pacific. They also had the same type of men aboard. Seawolf was named for the Atlantic wolffish, an aggressive predator of sea urchins and green crabs. The submarine proved just as aggressive a predator of Japanese ships.

Seawolf's war began on December 8, 1941. Seawolf was in the Philippines operating out of Cavite Naval Base in Manila Bay. Its captain was Lieutenant Commander Frederick B. Warder, who commissioned the boat and would serve as its skipper on its first seven war patrols. He took Seawolf out to patrol San Bernardino Strait within hours of the attack on Pearl Harbor. (The Philippines was on the far side of the International Date Line, so it was already December 8 for them when Pearl Harbor was bombed.)

On December 14, Warder moved Seawolf close inshore to attack a large Japanese ship, either a large transport or a tender, in Port San Vicente. Some of the torpedoes hit but failed to sink the ship. (The submarine service was plagued with faulty torpedoes, a problem that was not fully resolved until 1943.) In return, Seawolf went through a prolonged depth charging. Warder

Seawolf Park was named for USS *Seawolf* (SS-197) and is a memorial to that ship and all other U.S. Navy submarines lost at sea. *Seawolf* is shown here, shortly after entering service in 1939. *USNHHC.*

remained so calm during the Japanese counterattack that his men began calling him "Fearless Freddie."

Warder hated the nickname, but it stuck. He kept living up to it, remaining calm whenever *Seawolf* was under attack. After its first war patrol, *Seawolf* was sent to Australia, returning to the Philippines on its second patrol with a load of antiaircraft ammunition for Corregidor and only eight torpedoes aboard. After loading torpedoes at Corregidor, *Seawolf* patrolled the Java Sea near the Lombok Strait. In an aggressive patrol, *Seawolf* attacked seven ships, including a destroyer and three cruisers. It hit four, including two light cruisers and two cargo ships. It endured seven and a half hours being depth charged after hitting *Naka*, a *Sendai*-class light cruiser.

Seawolf's next four war patrols mirrored its first three. Warder conducted extremely aggressive patrols, attacking multiple ships on each patrol and sinking ships each time. Some patrols ended early, because *Seawolf* expended all torpedoes. At the end of *Seawolf*'s seventh war patrol, Lieutenant Commander Royce Gross relieved Warder. Warder went on to a well-earned promotion and bigger and better things, eventually becoming a rear admiral. *Seawolf* went to Mare Island, California, for a well-earned refit.

On returning to the Pacific, over the next four patrols, *Seawolf* under Gross continued the tradition it set under Warder, sinking numerous Japanese ships—in one patrol expending all of its torpedoes by the third day. At the end of the eleventh war patrol, on January 27, 1944, it went to Hunter's Point at San Francisco for another refit.

Seawolf returned to the Pacific in May, commanded by Richard Lynch. Now an older submarine, *Seawolf* began pulling special missions, freeing up new construction for war patrols against Japanese shipping. Seawolf conducted pre-invasion photography at Peleliu in June and July and was then transferred back to Australia, where it began clandestine missions running guerrillas and U.S. Army scouts into the Philippines.

It was carrying seventeen soldiers to Palawan in the Philippines on its fifteenth and final war patrol, with Albert Marion Bontier now commanding *Seawolf*. On October 3, 1944, *Seawolf*, underway to the Philippines, exchanged signals with *Narwhal*, also involved in the Philippine run. It was the last anyone would hear from *Seawolf*.

Seawolf proved one of the fightingest U.S. Navy submarines of World War II. This is a through-the-periscope photograph of one of Seawolf's victims, either SS *Gifu Maru* or Japanese gunboat *Keiko Maru*. *USNHHC.*

On October 3, the Japanese submarine *Ro-41* torpedoed and sank the destroyer escort *Shelton. Richard M. Rowell*, another destroyer escort in *Shelton's* group, went searching for its killer. It went after a submarine reported running surfaced by two carrier aircraft. The submarine submerged when the aircraft attacked it.

Rowell soon made sonar contact with the submarine. The submarine was in a safe lane. That meant *Rowell* should not attack unless it could be confirmed that the submarine was unfriendly. *Rowell* knew *Seawolf* would be transiting but failed to get the word that *Seawolf* was delayed. *Rowell's* captain assumed *Seawolf* was no longer in the area.

Rowell's sonar operator reported hearing a series of dots and dashes from the submerged target. It was probably *Seawolf*, which would have known any warship in the area was friendly, signaling its presence. A Japanese submarine would have gone silent, hoping to escape unobserved. *Rowell's* captain decided the signal was an attempt to "jam" his sonar. He attacked the submarine using his hedgehog, a deadly accurate system that dropped a ring of sixty-five-pound projectiles that exploded only when it contacted a target. Sonar reported explosions. Debris rose to the surface.

Ro-41 survived to fight another day. *Seawolf* disappeared, taking seventeen soldiers and eighty-two navy personnel with it. There was no report of any Japanese attack that could account for *Seawolf's* loss. It is possible *Seawolf* was lost due to an operational accident. More likely was that the last few minutes of those aboard were spent listening to an attack by a friendly warship.

14

DEATH IN THE MORNING

It started innocently as a small fire aboard a ship loading cargo in Texas City, Texas, on a mid-April day in 1947. By midnight on April 16, most of Texas City had been flattened, with at least 576 residents dead or missing. The results of the tragedy, known today as the Texas City Disaster, changed industrial safety laws in the United States, but it would haunt Texas City for the next seventy years.

Grandcamp arrived in Texas City on April 11, 1947. It was a Liberty ship, a class of cargo ship mass produced during World War II. Liberty ships displaced 14,245 tons, were 441.50 feet long and had a beam of 57.00 feet and a draft, fully loaded, of 27.75 feet. They could carry 10, 685 long tons of cargo. Liberty ships could steam at a maximum speed of 11.0 knots (11.5 with a clean hull) and had a range of 20,000 nautical miles traveling at the seven-knot speed of a slow World War II convoy. During World War II, 2,710 were built.

It was powered by old-fashioned but reliable triple-expansion steam engines. The steam went first through a high-pressure cylinder. The waste steam then passed through a medium-pressure cylinder and then a low pressure one. By the 1940s, triple-expansion engines, in use for sixty years, were being replaced by the more efficient steam turbine. The Liberty ship used the older design because they were available and reliable, while turbines were badly needed in warships.

Their boilers were fired by fuel oil, a grade known as Bunker-C. A heavy oil, it was barely refined from crude. Highly viscous at room temperatures,

An aerial view of Texas City following the explosion of *Grandcamp*. The devastation of the port and industrial section of Texas City is clearly shown. *UHDL.*

it was cheap and available. On Liberty ships, the fuel was stored in tanks adjacent to the cargo holds.

Grandcamp began life as *Benjamin R. Curtis*. Named for a deceased Supreme Court justice (all Liberty ships were named for American heroes), it was launched at the California Shipbuilding Corporation's Los Angeles shipyard on November 3, 1942. Laid up after the war, in January 1947, it was sold to the French government. They renamed it *Grandcamp*, after *Grandcamp-les-bains*, the Normandy invasion beach where Allied forces began the liberation of France in 1944.

Grandcamp was making its first voyage under a French flag when it arrived at Texas City, its last stop before returning to France. It had previously unloaded and loaded cargos in Cuba and Houston. Cargo aboard included 59,000 bales of sisal twine, 5,000 bales of tobacco, 933 bags of shelled peanuts, 380 bales of cotton and 280 boxes of oil well and farm equipment. There was also 2,400 pounds of small-arms ammunition aboard, stored in 16 crates. At Texas City, it was to pick up a load of ammonium nitrate fertilizer, badly needed in war-torn France. The ammonium nitrate being loaded on *Grandcamp* had been manufactured at U.S. Army explosive plants in Plains States during World War II. It is an ingredient used in the manufacture of explosives. Surplus, it was repurposed as fertilizer.

Ammonium nitrate is a common fertilizer. In the 1980s, backyard gardeners could buy bags of it to green up their plants. Ammonium nitrate burns. At the right combinations of temperature and pressure, it explodes. It becomes explosive when mixed with fuel oil. The agriculture department wrote advisories on how to mix up ammonium nitrate and diesel into ANFO (Ammonium Nitrate–Fuel Oil) explosives to give farmers a cheap way to blow stumps when clearing fields. An AFNO bomb destroyed the Alfred P. Murrah Federal Building in Oklahoma City on April 19, 1995.

That was decades in the future as longshoremen loaded one-hundred-pound bags of ammonium nitrate into *Grandcamp*'s Number 2 and 4 holds. No one thought of the cargo as explosive. Instead, it was viewed as inert, similar to bags of cement. The longshoremen received no special handling instructions. Smoking, almost universal in the 1940s, was permitted, and no special care was given to broken bags. They were loaded in with the rest. Loading began on April 11. By the time they stopped loading at 5:00 p.m. on April 15, 2,300 tons of fertilizer were aboard.

April 16, 1947, dawned unseasonably cool. It was fifty-six degrees. The first longshoremen boarded *Grandcamp* at 8:00 a.m., intent on finishing loading. They smelled smoke and soon saw smoke rising from the hold on the inshore side. Removing some bags, they soon saw a small fire deep in the hold. They tried but failed to extinguish the fire with four hand-held fire extinguishers and several jugs of drinking water. *Grandcamp*'s first officer, fearing water might damage the other cargo aboard, refused to permit its use to douse the fire. Instead, the hold was cleared of people and then sealed in an attempt to smother the fire. It failed.

A call for the fire department went out at 8:25 a.m. Two engines from the Texas City Volunteer Fire Department responded. By then, the fire was growing rapidly. Two more engines were dispatched, the rest of the small fire department. Soon all of its personnel were trying to extinguish the fire.

At this point, no one worried about the 2,300 tons of fertilizer exploding. Their concern centered on the 2,400 pounds of small arms ammunition. They started unloading those crates but were forced to stop as the fire increased. The crew of *Grandcamp* evacuated the ship. Its captain decided to flood the two holds filled with fertilizer with steam. His logic was that deprived of oxygen the fire would stop.

Devastation was widespread. This parking lot was over a quarter of a mile from Texas City's harbor. *UHDL.*

The plan had two problems. The first was that every molecule of ammonium nitrate contained three oxygen atoms. Once it started burning, it provided its own oxygen. The other problem was that hot ammonium nitrate reacts chemically with steam to create highly volatile nitic oxide. Filling the holds with steam literally pumped oxygen into the fire. Finally, there was a fuel bunker between holds 3 and 4, next to the blazing fertilizer. At the temperatures at which the fertilizer burned, if the fuel oil mixed with it, a spontaneous explosion would result.

At 9:12 a.m., thirty-seven minutes after the fire alarm sounded, the inevitable happened. Either the temperature in hold 4 reached 850 degrees, the explosion point of ammonium nitrate, or the bulkhead between the oil bunker and hold 4 failed, allowing fuel oil to mix with the burning ammonium nitrate. *Grandcamp* exploded.

The result was catastrophic. The detonation sent *Grandcamp*'s remaining cargo thousands of feet into the air. Burning fuel oil, bags of fertilizer, machinery, bales of twine and peanuts cascaded down on the harbor. So did molten bits of structural metal from *Grandcamp*. The blast created a fifteen-foot tidal wave that flooded the harbor. It flattened the buildings closest to *Grandcamp*, including the Monsanto chemical plant three hundred feet away and the warehouses and other buildings the Texas City Terminal Railways operated near the harbor. The shock wave shattered windows in Houston, forty miles away, and the explosion was felt as far away as Port Arthur, Texas.

The blast killed hundreds. Every man of the Texas City Volunteer Fire Department present was killed. So were workers in the nearby buildings. Bystanders were drawn to the scene by the unusual orange smoke billowing out of *Grandcamp*. Watching from what they thought was a safe distance, they were shredded. Thousands were injured.

Worse was yet to come. Flaming debris fell everywhere within a one-mile radius. *Grandcamp*'s anchor, one fluke missing, landed 1.6 miles from the ship. A 150-foot by 28-foot steel barge near *Grandcamp* was picked up and dropped 100 feet inland from where it was moored. Pieces of debris, some burning, punched through roofs of buildings throughout Texas City, starting fires and making homes uninhabitable. Two other ships in Texas City's harbor, *Wilson B. Keene* and *Highflyer*, both operated by the Lykes Line, were damaged by the explosion. *Highflyer*, on the side of the pier opposite *Grandcamp*, was pushed into *Wilson B. Keene* as its mooring lines parted.

Texas City was in a desperate state. There were fires starting all over town, but it no longer had a fire department. All four fire engines and all but one of its men had been killed when *Grandcamp* exploded. There were thousands injured but no hospital in Texas City. Local heavy construction equipment was inoperable, damaged in the blast.

Locals who survived the blast began responding. A telephone operator's strike had muted Texas City's telephones, but on hearing what happened, the operators returned to work. Texas City was filled with oil and chemical plants that developed disaster response plans intended for an emergency in their own facilities. They dealt with their immediate problems, but once under control, they assisted their immediate neighbors and then the general community. Texas City's power and water were both knocked out by the blast. Emergency generators and portable pumps were used to fight fires.

Texas City's ordeal was not over. *Highflyer* had been in the pier directly adjacent to *Grandcamp*. After *Highflyer*'s mooring lines snapped, the anchor was dropped to keep the ship from drifting. Although *Highflyer* was moored with its bows pointed to the sea, its engine was inoperable. It had been partly disassembled for a routine maintenance inspection. *Grandcamp*'s explosion blew *Highflyer*'s hatch covers off, knocked out *Highflyer*'s electricity, buckled

Wilson B. Keene sunk in Texas City's harbor the day after the Texas City disaster. Battered by the explosion of *Grandcamp*, its hull was shattered when *Highflyer* exploded next to it. *UHDL.*

decks and ruptured steam lines. It drifted out of its berths fetching up alongside *Wilson B. Keene*, ahead of it on the pier. *Highflyer* also carried a load of ammonium nitrate, 1,000 tons worth. It also carried 2,000 tons of sulfur, a chemical that interacts with and increases the volatility of ammonium nitrate. *Highlfyer*, too, caught fire.

Tugboats were called to tow the blazing *Highflyer* out of the harbor, away from Texas City. They could not get the ship out of its berth. The ship stubbornly refused to move, blocked in place by submerged debris. Containing the fire was impossible. After trying since 8:00 p.m. to move *Highflyer*, the effort was abandoned shortly after midnight. Its crew evacuated and the area was cleared to the extent possible. Finally, at 1:10 a.m. on April 17, *Highflyer* exploded.

The blast sank *Wilson B. Keene*, only a few feet from *Highflyer* and already battered from the previous explosion. It demolished the pier to which *Keene* was moored and flattened the few buildings still standing after the earlier explosion. It rained more flaming debris and metal shards on Texas City.

Since it was expected, everyone had taken cover. Only two additional deaths could be directly attributed to it. The port was already so badly smashed that it was hard to determine what additional damage the second blast caused.

Help came pouring into Texas City. Neighboring towns sent fire engines, firefighters and ambulances. Much of the early aid was sent unasked. The sheer size of the explosion sent up a massive cloud of smoke, and the shockwave let everyone in surrounding communities realize Texas City had been hit hard and needed help.

The army mobilized, sending equipment and men to help. So did the coast guard, navy and Texas National Guard. Galveston, Houston and San Antonio sent police officers to help the Texas City Police Department maintain order. Hundreds of volunteers, some teenage Boy Scouts and Girl Scouts, flooded into Texas City from Galveston and Houston. The Red Cross responded and was soon coordinating the efforts of four thousand volunteers.

With no hospital in Texas City, triage centers were set up in city hall and the chamber of commerce building. Those seriously wounded were evacuated to John Sealy Hospital in Galveston, Fort Crockett's hospital and the many hospitals in Houston. The high school gymnasium was used as a temporary morgue and a local auto shop was used as an embalming facility. The Red Cross established emergency centers for residents whose homes were uninhabitable, providing victims with food, water and shelter.

The U.S. Coast Guard report on the incident listed 433 known dead and 128 reported missing. Many were the spectators drawn to the scene by the fire. The death toll could be higher. The explosion obliterated many of the victims. Remains of only four members of the Texas City Volunteer Fire Department known to be present were found. There were foreign sailors and transient workers whose presence were unrecorded and not listed among the known missing. Eventually, the casualty would rise to 576 known dead, with 78 unidentified. Another 178 were missing, presumed dead.

Texas City eventually recovered. Monsanto, then the city's largest employer, rebuilt its plant, which had been flattened in the explosions. The coast guard and federal government implemented new regulations for handling hazardous cargoes, especially ammonium nitrate. These included restrictions on smoking near flammable cargoes. New industrial safety regulations went into play. Even before that, the industries in Texas City developed the Industrial Mutual Aid System (IMAS) to help each other in the event of disaster and coordinate response.

Lawsuits followed for years. Since the ammonium nitrate originated from federal government plants, the federal government was a defendant.

The explosion threw *Grandcamp*'s anchor 1.6 miles. It is now on display at Texas City Memorial Park, next to the cemetery where many of the unidentified dead from the Texas City disaster are buried. *Author photograph.*

Ultimately, the Supreme Court ruled in the government's favor in 1953, accepting the argument that the government enjoyed sovereign immunity. Congress voted on a relief bill three years later, providing $16 million in compensation. The last lawsuit, against the government of France, finally ended in 1962, when the Supreme Court refused to hear an appeal against a lower court ruling absolving the French government.

The work of identifying the dead went on for months. The city held its first memorial service on Saturday, April 19. A multidenominational service was conducted at the high school football stadium, with over one thousand attending. On June 22, 1947, the bodies of the unidentified victims were buried in a mass ceremony at a small cemetery on Texas City's north side. Today, it is the site of the Memorial Park, filled with monuments, statues and plaques honoring the dead. A visitor can feel the pain the event had caused.

15

THE GHOST CAPTAIN

OF THE *TEXAS*

So far, this book has discussed many figurative ghosts but few literal ones—as in haunts, the spirits of those who have passed over but whose spirit stubbornly refuses to leave this earthly vale remaining behind to remind people of their presence on Earth. If you have an imagination, you can feel the spirit of Cabeza de Vaca or the sailors lost aboard the 1554 treasure fleet as you walk the patch of coast on which they wrecked.

Standing at Sabine Pass, you can almost hear Dick Dowling chuckling as he a goes to accept the surrender of the Union fleet. You cannot help feeling haunted by those who died at Texas City when you visit its memorial park. Visiting Seawolf Park and standing by the *Seawolf* Monument and the Memorial Circle, you can wonder what the sailors and soldiers aboard the submarine *Seawolf* must have felt as depth charges launched by U.S. destroyers rained down on them. But what about a real ghost? A real haunting?

Ghosts are really popular, it seems. People love to read about ghosts, visit haunted places and speculate about haunts. Just about everyone has a ghost story they like to share. Several ships have ghosts. The best known (in Texas at least) is the Essex-class aircraft carrier *Lexington*, now a museum ship in Corpus Christi. It even had a ghost cam set up in the engine room to catch the apparition. Having a ghost aboard your ship is good publicity.

The state's most famous museum ship is the battleship *Texas*. It served the United States Navy for forty-four years before finally being retired as a museum ship in its namesake state in 1948. Except for a brief patch in the 1990s, when it was sent to Todd Shipyard in Galveston for a refit, it has been

The final U.S. Navy crew of BB-35, USS *Texas*. The picture was taken on arrival at the San Jacinto Battlefield Park. John McKeown is fourth from the left in the front row of standing men. *TPWD.*

there ever since. It is scheduled to depart for another overhaul and will likely be relocated elsewhere when it returns to Texas. As of the writing of this book, it remains at its slip at the San Jacinto Battlefield, however.

Does *Texas* have a resident ghost? If you ask the staff of the battleship, none recall seeing a ghost aboard the ship or even hearing a tale of a ghostly presence on *Texas*. That is unsurprising. According to ghost hunters, there must be a good reason to haunt a place. A strong trauma or long association has to exist for a mortal's spirit to remain at a place after death.

Texas led a pretty staid existence during its years as a U.S. Navy warship, retiring in 1946. Since 1948, it has been moored at the San Jacinto Battlefield Park, a monument to the men of Texas who served in World War I and World War II. Texas schoolkids helped raise money to move the battleship to a berth at the San Jacinto Monument.

Even before World War I, it had exciting times. Its first deployment saw it support the U.S. occupation of Veracruz, Mexico, in 1914, supporting the landing made by U.S. Marines. Later, on May 27, 1915, before the United States entered World War I, *Texas* participated in a dramatic rescue in the Atlantic. The Dutch steamship *Ryndam* collided with another ship off Nantucket. *Texas* assisted the crew and passengers of the steamer. *Ryndam*'s owners, the Holland-American Line, gratefully presented *Texas* with a silver model of the seventeenth-century Dutch admiral de Ruyter's flagship, *De Zeven Provincien*, for this accomplishment. But nobody died at Veracruz or during the *Ryndam* rescue, so there was no trauma to attach a ghost to *Texas*.

During World War I, the British Grand Fleet (led by *Texas*, incidentally) encountered the German High Seas Fleet off Norway in 1918. It was the last time the two fleets would meet, and the outnumbered Germans turned tail and ran. *Texas* saw the tail-end of the German fleet as it scampered back to port. Again, no casualties.

Between the wars, *Texas* led the staid life of a peacetime U.S. Navy battleship. It served as a flagship in both the Atlantic and Pacific fleets, carried President Coolidge to Havana for the Pan-American conference in 1928 and went through numerous refits. Its crew spent most of its time keeping the ship spick and span. There were a few exciting events. It became the first U.S. Navy battleship to launch an aircraft. There was nothing that would have created a trauma ghost.

In World War II, *Texas* served three years in the Atlantic before finishing the war in the Pacific. *Texas* escorted convoys early in the war. It was part of the Neutrality Patrol in the Western North Atlantic in 1940 and 1941. In June 1941, when the United States was still neutral, *Texas* was almost torpedoed by *U-203*. Fortunately, the German U-boat did not line up the shot. If it had, World War II's rallying cry might have been "Remember the *Texas*" instead of "Remember Pearl Harbor."

Later, *Texas* provided gunnery support at North Africa, Normandy, Cherbourg, southern France, Iwo Jima and Okinawa. During that whole time, it only had one man killed in combat. Save for one battle, off Cherbourg, when a pair of German shells struck it, it went through the war untouched. Even at Cherbourg, one of the shells was a dud. (It is now on display at the battleship.) Do not look to its navy service for a haunting.

Having a good ghost aboard would be an attraction. It provides one more reason to visit on October 31. If there was a ghost haunting *Texas*, it has to be a long-association ghost.

There is a first-class candidate for an official Ghost of the Battleship *Texas*: John "Tiger Jack" McKeown.

McKeown was a thirty-year navy man. McKeown served thirteen of those years on *Texas* when it was a U.S. Navy warship both before and during World War II. He retired from the U.S. Navy in 1948 as a machinist's mate-chief petty officer. His last assignment before retiring was aboard *Texas*. He was part of the crew that rode the ship from Baltimore, Maryland, where

For many years, McKeown served as *Texas*'s superintendent. He called himself "captain" of the *Texas* and frequently greeted visitors, especially navy veterans from World War II dressed in his self-designed Texas Navy captain's uniform. *TPWD.*

it had been laid up, to the San Jacinto Battlefield off the Houston Ship Channel in Texas.

After the handover ceremony in 1948, McKeown returned to Norfolk, Virginia, to receive his discharge. But the old battleship called to him. McKeown headed back to Houston to take a job as one of two assistant caretakers for the battleship. His tenure as an assistant caretaker was brief. Within six months, the other assistant caretaker and the caretaker were dismissed after having tangled with the Lloyd Gregory, then the head of the Battleship *Texas* Commission. McKeown was named caretaker, a job he would hold for the next twenty-one years.

McKeown soon abandoned the title of caretaker of the *Texas*. He proclaimed himself to be the "captain" of the *Texas*. During working hours, he wore a uniform. It can be called a captain's uniform only for the third Texas Navy, the one that never officially existed. It bore only incidental resemblance to any uniform of the United States Armed Forces. It was made up of bits and pieces of different uniforms. He wore a chief petty officer's coat with captain's rank insignia on it. He topped it with a white U.S. Army officer's hat, with the U.S. Army device on the front replaced by the seal of the State of Texas. It was improbable and colorful. The former CPO reveled in wearing it.

The caretaker's job also included free housing. In 1948, there was a small house next to the *Texas* for its superintendent. Instead, McKeown decided to live on the ship. He moved into the captain's quarters—a four-room suite on the superstructure deck, the most spacious accommodation on the ship. It was grander than the stateroom in petty officers' quarters he shared when he was aboard *Texas* in his closing days in the navy and far better than the compartment he had slung a hammock in as a sailor. (Even into the 1930s and World War II, ordinary sailors slept in hammocks aboard *Texas*.) It was his home for the next twenty-two years.

McKeown spent the next two decades a happy man. As he was a bachelor with no known relatives, the ship became home to McKeown and his family: three toy bulldogs, Jiggs, Pogo and Pat. They lived aboard ship with him, and he spoiled them badly. When McKeown fixed himself a steak, he could not serve his dogs hamburger. He had to fix a separate steak for each of them.

McKeown and his dogs became as much of a fixture aboard the ship as its guns and engine. Children who visited *Texas* were delighted by his dogs. McKeown was a great favorite with visitors, who would come to hear his sea stories. He loved swapping memories with other veteran sailors who visited *Texas*. He was always ready to pose for a photo with an old shipmate aboard *Texas*. As far as McKeown was concerned, if you served in the U.S. Navy, especially during "The Big One"—World War II—you were a shipmate, even if you had never served aboard a ship with McKeown or even a ship on which McKeown had served.

He was five foot seven and broad-shouldered with bright blue eyes and a peppery temperament. He enjoyed playing the role of an irascible Irishman. While some of the sea stories he told might not have been real, what was real was his abiding love for *Texas*. He never married, but in a real sense, was married to *Texas*. To McKeown, it was "my ship." *Texas* employees reported that McKeown roamed the lower decks of *Texas* at night. Completely familiar with the ship, he moved about in the dark, with no lights. When nightwatchmen encountered him, he would tell them "his old lady was talking to him." When interviewed by the press, McKeown frequently stated that he wanted to "die on the ship." It was truly the great love of his life.

He did not quite achieve that goal. In late 1969, he became too ill to continue his service. He was diagnosed with stomach cancer and hospitalized. Another World War II naval veteran was named McKeown's replacement as *Texas*'s "captain." Yet McKeown's heart remained with *Texas*. Wracked with pain as he lay in bed dying of cancer, his eyes lit up whenever he spoke of "my ship." He continued to worry about "his lady."

McKeown meets with the Battleship *Texas* board in the captain's suite aboard the Battleship *Texas* during the late 1960s. *TPWD.*

On cold days, he would tell friends from *Texas* who visited him to "be sure to drain the ship's water lines."

Finally, on February 11, 1970, stomach cancer defeated Tiger Jack, and he died. Even in his final illness, his thoughts were on the ship. His will directed that he be cremated and asked for his ashes to be scattered in the waters around the *Texas. Texas* arrived at its San Jacinto Battlefield berth on San Jacinto Day, April 21. Ever since, *Texas* observed San Jacinto Days with festivities, celebrations and ceremonies. On San Jacinto Day in 1970, sixty-nine days after McKeown's death, his wishes were honored. In a memorial ceremony, his ashes were committed to the waters around *Texas*'s berth. Even in death, McKeown remained with his lady.

No one is saying there is a ghost on the *Texas*. After all, everyone knows there is no such things as ghosts. But if there was a ghost, it would be Tiger Jack, standing watch over his old ship. Including his time aboard *Texas* when he was in the navy, he lived nearly half of his life aboard the ship. He was possessed by the ship during the last two decades of his life. He refused to be parted from the ship even after death.

John McKeown in his quarters aboard the *Texas* late in his career. *Texas* was the true love of his life. It would not be strange if his spirit was still aboard. *TPWD.*

There are reports of things moved around on *Texas*: misplaced objects mysteriously restored to their proper location and litter collected before the staff can get to it. All of this can be explained by ordinary means. Or perhaps it could be explained by a friendly spirit, the soul of a man who used to wander the ship at night, so familiar with it that he could move about in the dark, without light, who was obsessed with seeing that things remain ship-shaped.

If you are on the *Texas* late at night, you might catch the scent of a Chesterfield (on a tobacco-free ship) or hear what sounds for the world like the bark of a small bulldog. Perhaps you might hear echoing footsteps where no one is supposed to be or see lights through the windows of the captain's cabin—lights that disappear when you go over there to check.

It is probably just your imagination. It could not possibly be Tiger Jack checking on his old ship.

Right?

BIBLIOGRAPHY

Bandelier, Ad. F., ed. and trans. *The Journey of Álvar Núñez Cabeza de Vaca and His Companions from Florida to the Pacific 1528–1536*. New York: Allerton Book Co., 1922.

Blair, Clay Jr. *Silent Victory: The US Submarine War Against Japan*. Philadelphia: J.B. Lippincott Company, 1975.

Bricker, Richard W. *Wooden Ships from Texas: A World War Saga*. College Station: University of Texas A&M Press, 1998.

Cormier, George Anne. *Indianola Visitors Guide*. Port Lavaca, TX: Calhoun County Museum, 2008.

Davis, William C. *The Pirates Laffite: The Treacherous World of the Corsairs of the Gulf*. Orlando, FL: Harcourt, 2005.

Foster, William C., ed. *The La Salle Expedition to Texas: The Journal of Henri Joutel, 1684–1687*. Austin: Texas State Historical Association, 1998.

Handbook of Texas. State Historical Association. https://www.tshaonline.org/handbook.

Jordan, Jonathan W. *Lone Star Navy: Texas, the Fight for the Gulf of Mexico, and the Shaping of the American West*. Washington, D.C.: Potomac Books, 2006.

U.S. Coast Guard. *Record of Proceeding of Board of Investigation Inquiring into Losses by Fires and Explosions of the French Steamship* Grandcamp *and US Steamships* Highflyer *and* Wilson B. Keene *at Texas City 16 and 17 April 1947*. Washington D.C, 1947.

Wells, Tom Henderson. *Commodore Moore and the Texas Navy*. Austin: University of Texas Press, 1960.

INDEX

ABOUT THE AUTHOR

 **M**ark Lardas, a sometime engineer, freelance writer, historian and model-maker, has lived in the Houston area for forty years. He is currently employed as a technical writer and spends his spare time collecting offbeat stories about Texas and maritime history. He worked on the Shuttle program as a navigator and engineer from 1979 until 2011.